How to Play
Racquet Ball, Paddle Ball & Platform Tennis

N. MacLean

Other books of interest

How To Play Badminton, Pat Davis, Coles Publishing Co. Ltd., Toronto, 1977

Play Squash, Tony Swift, Coles Publishing Co. Ltd., Toronto, 1975

Racquet Sports, The Diagram Group, Coles Publishing Co. Ltd., Toronto, 1978

Starting Squash, Dick Hawkey, Coles Publishing Co. Ltd., Toronto, 1975

Teach Yourself Badminton, Ken Crossley, Coles Publishing Co. Ltd., Toronto, 1976

Winning Badminton, Alex T. Watson, Coles Publishing Co. Ltd., Toronto, 1976

Winning Squash, Claire Chapman, Coles Publishing Co. Ltd., Toronto, 1976

© COPYRIGHT 1980 AND PUBLISHED BY
COLES PUBLISHING COMPANY LIMITED
TORONTO – CANADA
PRINTED IN CANADA

contents

Chapter 1 BACKGROUND / 11

Chapter 2 COURT TENNIS / 31

Chapter 3 RACQUETBALL / 39

Chapter 4 HOW TO PLAY RACQUETBALL / 55

Chapter 5 PADDLEBALL / 71

Chapter 6 HOW TO PLAY PADDLEBALL / 83

Chapter 7 PLATFORM TENNIS / 95

Chapter 8 HOW TO PLAY PLATFORM TENNIS / 107

Chapter 9 BUILDING A PLATFORM TENNIS COURT / 123

Acknowledgements are gratefully given to

Gloria Dillenbeck

and

Tribuno Wines, Inc., Sponsors of the Tribuno Platform Tennis Circuit.

To my father
who first interested me in sports

How to Play
Racquet Ball, Paddle Ball & Platform Tennis

chapter 1

Background

MANY A HISTORY STUDENT is familiar with the story of the French king Louis X who died in 1316 after contracting a chill on "the tennis court."

What most of these students don't know is that the game the king was playing wasn't the tennis the vast majority of people either play or watch on television. In fact, Louis X would not recognize today's game of tennis any more than he would recognize television. What he was playing was a game still known today in many parts of Europe as tennis, but what is called "court tennis" in North America. States.

Court tennis (or Royal Tennis) is the ancestor of the modern game of tennis which was invented in 1874 in England by Walter Clopton Wingfield, a retired British Army major. The origins of the parent game of court tennis are somewhat obscure, but its prestige is universal enough so that the game North Americans call "tennis" is called "lawn tennis" by many others. This distinguishes it from court tennis, which has been shortened to "tennis" by enthusiasts (and sticklers for form) outside of North America.

Louis X wasn't the only leader of fads and styles in Europe devoted to playing court tennis. The aristocracy, as well, was quite taken with the game and all of the world's court tennis courts are designed exactly as the ancient courts were, creating a bizarre environment for the game.

The basic court is divided into two halves by the net. The halves are the service end and the hazard end, although the term "hazard end" could honestly be applied to the whole game! The floor is divided by lines which are known as "chases" creating targets for balls to be hit into. The walls are surrounded on three of the four sides by a sloping roof and both the walls and the penthouse contain various openings and obstructions including the dedans, the tambour, the grille and the galleries.

The tambour is a jutting object on the left wall of the hazard end and is thought to represent the flying buttress of the monastery, the galleries and their posts on the facing long wall provide an opening to view through, but are thought to represent cowsheds and other agricultural buildings, the grille opening in the end of the hazard may represent a buttery hatch.

The sloping shed-like roof around the three walls, known as the penthouse, represents the mercantile or cloister buildings.

In this manner, representations of the entire society were incorporated into the medieval game of court tennis.

Courts along this line were constructed indoors as early as 1230 in recorded history in France, and probably much earlier. The game became so popular that even when it was frowned upon by the church at different times in both France and England, its popularity was not damaged. Later, in 1401 and 1414, the Dutch sought to prohibit its playing with similar lack of success.

Henry VIII, on the other hand, promoted court construction in England and built three of the most famous—St. James' Palace, Whitehall and Hampton Courts. The ravages of fire and time wiped out the first two, but the third remains as the oldest active court in the world today and has been used for the world championship challenges in this century.

The court itself is a rectangle 110 feet long and 38 feet wide. This area is enclosed by four cement walls 30 feet high with a cement-like floor below. On this floor are the markings referred to earlier. They begin at the service end a half-yard from the dedans wall (behind the server) and extend at 18-inch intervals to the beginning of the galleries.

After the 12 stripes marking off the first six yards in half-yard intervals comes the chase marked "a half yard worse than 6" and then "one yard worse than 6," "the second gallery," "the door" and "the first gallery" which are self explanatory in that they refer to openings in the wall to the left of the service court.

Then comes the net and beyond it, on the hazard side, are more markings which include "hazard chase first gallery," "hazard chase the door," "hazard chase the second gallery," "hazard chase two yards," "hazard chase one and two," "hazard chase one yard" and "hazard chase half a yard" which is followed by the service line. The remainder of the hazard area is unmarked except for a "pass line" parallel to the tambour extending from the service line to the back wall of the hazard court. There is of course, a service line on the roof as well.

Court tennis itself was an outgrowth and refinement of racquet, stick and bat ball games which retreat even further into antiquity.

These games, played with a ball, are almost as old as the recorded history of man. They were known to be popular sports among the Phoenicians, Romans, Greeks, Incas, Mayans and many other ancient civilizations.

The Greeks and Romans played a game similar to court tennis and built courts to accommodate such a game. As a result, it is reasonable to say that court tennis was the father of the many varieties of racquet stick and ball games which we know today.

Exactly how the game of court tennis came to France is not precisely known, but one reasonable theory is that in the 11th or 12th century it returned with the crusaders who had freed Jerusalem from the infidels. Once a playable version of court tennis was taken up by French royalty, it was immediately embraced by the aristocracy and the term "court" could then be applied with equal truth to the place where the game was played as well as to the kind of player who played it.

Once the game became established with the upper classes in France, it became the rage of the monied but untitled man. By the thirteenth century, Paris was filled with court tennis fanatics and over 1400 courts were built for playing the game. These courts varied only somewhat in size and shape, heights of the walls, the length and width of the playing floor had to be adjusted to the available space within the building containing the court.

One nobleman (Phillippe de Bel, in 1308) is known to have purchased a hotel simply to obtain the court within for his own convenience and this doubtless happened on more than one occasion. Suffice to say that court tennis was *the* game of the French at the time the unfortunate Louis took his chill and died. The game at the time was played both outdoors and indoors. Perhaps because of the death of the king, the indoor game began to become predominant among the French and it was more or less established as an indoor game when it became popular with the English.

Intermarriage between the French and English royal families may well have spurred interest in the game in Britain. By the time of the Tudors, court tennis was the royal game of England, as well. Henry VIII, an enthusiastic follower, gave the game even greater popularity when he ascended the throne of England in 1509.

Peter Garnier of Poitiers, France, is supposed to have built the first indoor court for tennis sometime around the year 1200, and over three hundred years later there were literally thousands of indoor court tennis courts in northern Europe and England. Then the game fell into disfavor with the majority of its followers when gambling scandals were exposed soon after professional matches were held. Betting was popular and the wagers ruinously high. The professionals were bribed and soon the game became a cynical charade for gambling.

Nevertheless, the aristocracy still clung to the game and when the first official rules were set down by Forbet in France in 1592, the game was well on the road to recovery.

Court tennis all but disappeared in England, however, during the revolution of 1649 which cost Charles I his head and brought Oliver Cromwell, with his puritanical views on games, to the head of the English government. The restoration of the monarchy with Charles II and the Stuarts in 1660 began a steady revival of games, including court tennis, in England.

The fall of Louis XVI in 1793, his subsequent execution and the rise of the French revolutionaries, who banished anything tainted by being associated with royalty and the aristocracy, lead to the virtual disappearance of court tennis in France.

The high cost of building and maintaining the indoor courts in accordance with the historic regulations also did much to reduce the game's popularity. In addition, the complex rules made it difficult for the less well educated to familiarize themselves with court tennis. The fact that the game, by 1700, was played almost entirely indoors also reduced its popularity and the steadily-diminishing number of available courts restricted play to those of influence. The less fortunate man began to look elsewhere for his recreation.

Today, there are less than 40 court tennis courts in the world. They largely exist in Australia, England, France, Canada, and the United States. Those in America are located in New York, Philadelphia, Boston, Tuxedo Park, New York, Aiken, South Carolina, and total seven in number.

The game retained its popularity with the rich and titled well into the 20th century, but the rise of the middle class brought about by World War I virtually reduced it to a unique status. Oddly enough, the first world championship court tennis match was not held until 1885 when Thomas Pettitt, an Englishman living in Boston, won the crown by defeating George Lambert, an English professional, 7 sets to 5, at England's Hampton Court. After Pettitt retired, Peter Latham of London (the holder of the world title in racquets since 1887) challenged Charles Sanders for the title. Sanders had been defeated by Pettitt, 7 sets to 5, in Dublin in 1890.

In 1896, Latham defeated Sanders for the championship and, two years later, Pettitt came out of competitive retirement to challenge him for the crown. But Pettitt was well past the peak of his game and was routed by Latham, 7 sets to none. Another Londoner, Cecil (Punch) Fairs, deposed Latham in 1905 but Latham won the title back in 1907 before being again deposed by Fairs the following year.

G.F. Covey continued the London monopoly on the world title when he succeeded Fairs in 1912. But then Jay Gould, a Philadelphian and scion of the famous railroad family, became the first amateur and first native-born American to win the crown.

Gould held the United States championship in court tennis almost continuously from 1906 to 1925 and was a partner in championship doubles teams well into the 1930's. He was clearly the dominant force in the game during the era between the two World Wars. He gained the world championship in 1914 when he defeated Covey, 7 sets to 3. Gould retired from international competition in 1916 although he nominally held the title because there were no challenges made due to the disruption of the first World War.

Then, in 1922, Covey beat Walter Kinsella of the United States, 7 sets to 3, to regain the title and successfully defended it against Kinsella in 1923. Covey also turned back the challenge of Pierre Etchebaster, a French Basque, in 1927, winning 7 of 11 sets. But a new era was dawning in court tennis and Etchebaster defeated Covey in 1928, 7 sets out of 10, to win the world title.

Of the three great champions of the game in the modern era, Pettitt's shots were legend and he was considered the most difficult man to defeat who ever played the game. When he reigned as the world champion, the game was more universally popular than in later years and many of the men who in subsequent generations were diverted to other sports were in the field to challenge Pettitt and few did so with success. Gould never lost a competition singles match and only once was on the losing side in a competition doubles game. But during much of his reign the field of competitors was steadily shrinking and few new players of international caliber were being developed, a fact of which Gould was aware and one reason why he retired.

However, there is little doubt that Etchebaster was the equal of Pettitt and Gould. During the height of his career, Etchebaster was an incredible shotmaker and an indefatigable opponent. He won his five international challenges in the era following World War II by the incredible margin of 35 sets to 9 against the finest competition from

North America and Great Britain. In toto, Etchebaster held the world championship for a record 27 years, accepting and meeting all challenges from legitimate champions of other countries until his retirement in 1955.

James Dear, an English professional who had given Etchebaster his most difficult challenges, became the champion upon his retiring by defeating another Britisher, Albert B. Johnson, in a classic match, 11 sets to 10, in London in 1955. In 1957, Johnson again challenged the aging Dear and beat him, 7 sets to 3. But the next year, an American, Northrup R. Knox, challenged and defeated Johnson to bring the title back to the United States where it has remained for nearly 20 years. This ancient antecedent of lawn tennis and numerous other games in North America will be discussed further in chapter 8.

One of the first outgrowths of court tennis was jai alai, a creation universally acknowledged to have been made by the Basques of the French and Spanish Pyrenees Mountains in the 17th century. Jai alai is a three-walled game played with a hard ball and a long basket-type racquet. The Basque terms are *pelota* for the ball and *cesta* for the racquet.

However, jai alai remained almost exclusively Basque until early in this century when it finally began to spread into Mexico, the Philippines and the United States. Florida legalized parimutuel wagering on jai alai in 1931 and since then courts have sprung up in Miami, Daytona Beach, Tampa and other Florida cities where there are large numbers of Spanish and Latin American immigrants. Tourists soon became addicted to the fast game as well as the legalized betting. In recent years, jai alai has spread to other parts of the United States, largely because Americans, now traveling extensively throughout Latin America, Spain and Portugal, have enjoyed watching the game and have learned its rules. However, even today most of the top 200 players in the world remain Basques.

Another variant of court tennis was to become more popular in its day than its parent sport: that was the game of racquets, created in the Fleet Street Debtors Jail in London by bored prisoners in the early 19th century. A former prisoner, Robert McKay, became the first recognized champion in 1820. Many of the other imprisoned debtors, once released, retained their fervor for the new game and their enthusiasm soon caught on. It took hold at Harrow, the famous exclusive school near London and its students soon were devoted to the game. Shortly, it was being played at other expensive schools such as Rugby (birthplace of another outdoor game of some vigor)

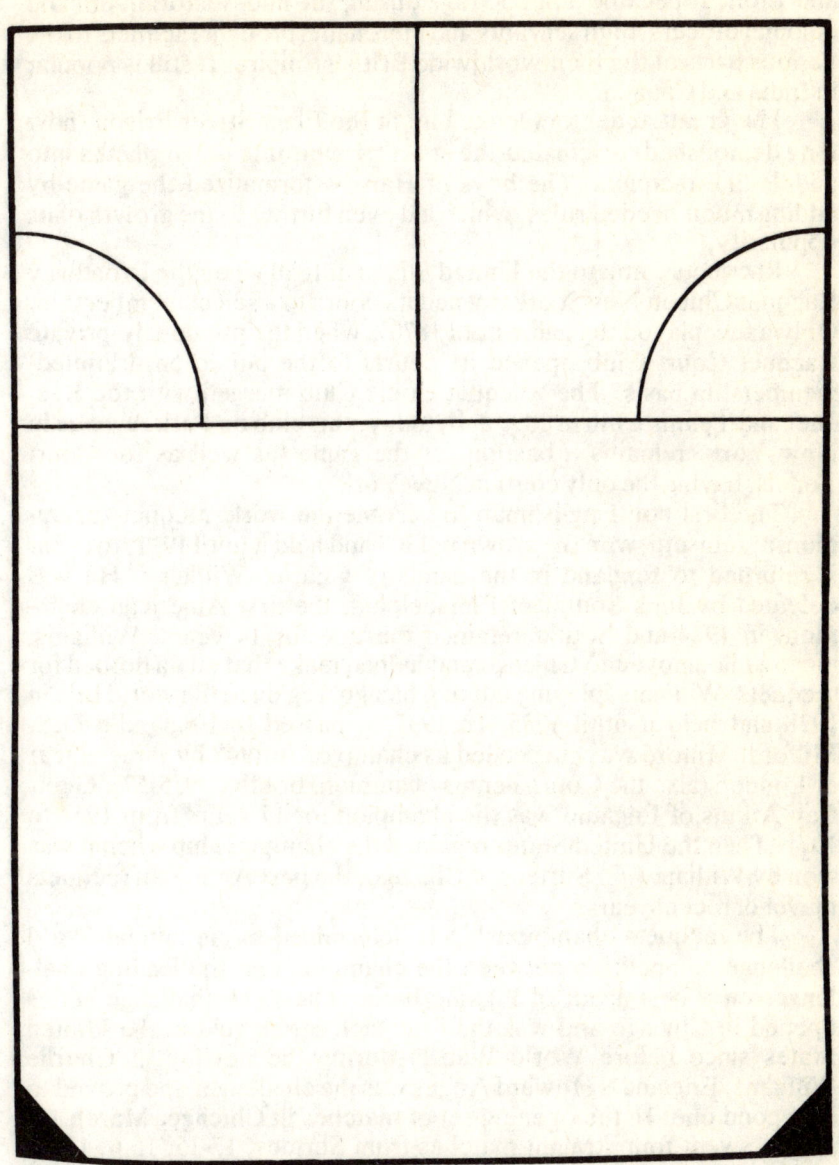

Official Squash Court

and Eton. It became a public rage during the mid-Victorian era and colonial officers, civil servants and merchants brought racquets to the various parts of the then-worldwide British Empire. It still is popular in India and Canada.

The creative debtors locked up in the Fleet Street Prison (now long demolished) originated the sport by whittling down planks into paddle-like racquets. The boys of Harrow formalized the game by adding much-needed rules, which led even further to the growth of its popularity.

Racquets came to the United States in 1850 when the Broadway Racquet Club in New York opened its doors to a select membership. Only a few played the game until 1870's when the previously-private Racquet Court Club opened its courts to the public on a limited-membership basis. The Racquet Court Club merged with the Racquet and Tennis Club in 1890 and, today, this club on Park Avenue in New York, remains a bastion for the game (as well as for Court Tennis, having the only court in New York).

The first non-Englishman to become the world racquets champion, J. Jamsetji, won the crown in 1903 and held it until 1911, the year it returned to England in the hands of Charles Williams. He was defeated by Jock Soutar of Philadelphia, the first American champion, in 1914 and Soutar retained the title for 14 years. Williams, meanwhile, moved to Chicago and helped make that city a hotbed for racquets. Williams, playing out of Chicago, regained the world title in 1928 and held it until 1935. In 1937, it passed to England's D.S. Milford. Milford was succeeded as champion in 1947 by James Dear of London (also the Court Tennis champion, briefly, 1955-57). Geoffrey Atkins of England was the champion for 17 years from 1954 to 1971. Then the United States regained the championship when it was won by William J.C. Surtees of Chicago, the best American racquets player of recent years.

The racquets championship is determined by an annual world challenge competition between the champion and the leading challenger on a best 5 out of 9 game basis. The 1973 challenge series opened in Chicago and was the first such series held in the United States since before World War II during the heyday of Charlie Williams. England's Howard Angus was the challenger and proved to be a good one. In the opening set of matches in Chicago, March 17, Angus swept four straight matches from Surtees, 17-15, 15-6, 15-12 and 15-5. The series then shifted to London for the final four matches, if necessary, with Angus holding a 4-0 edge. Surtees won the opening

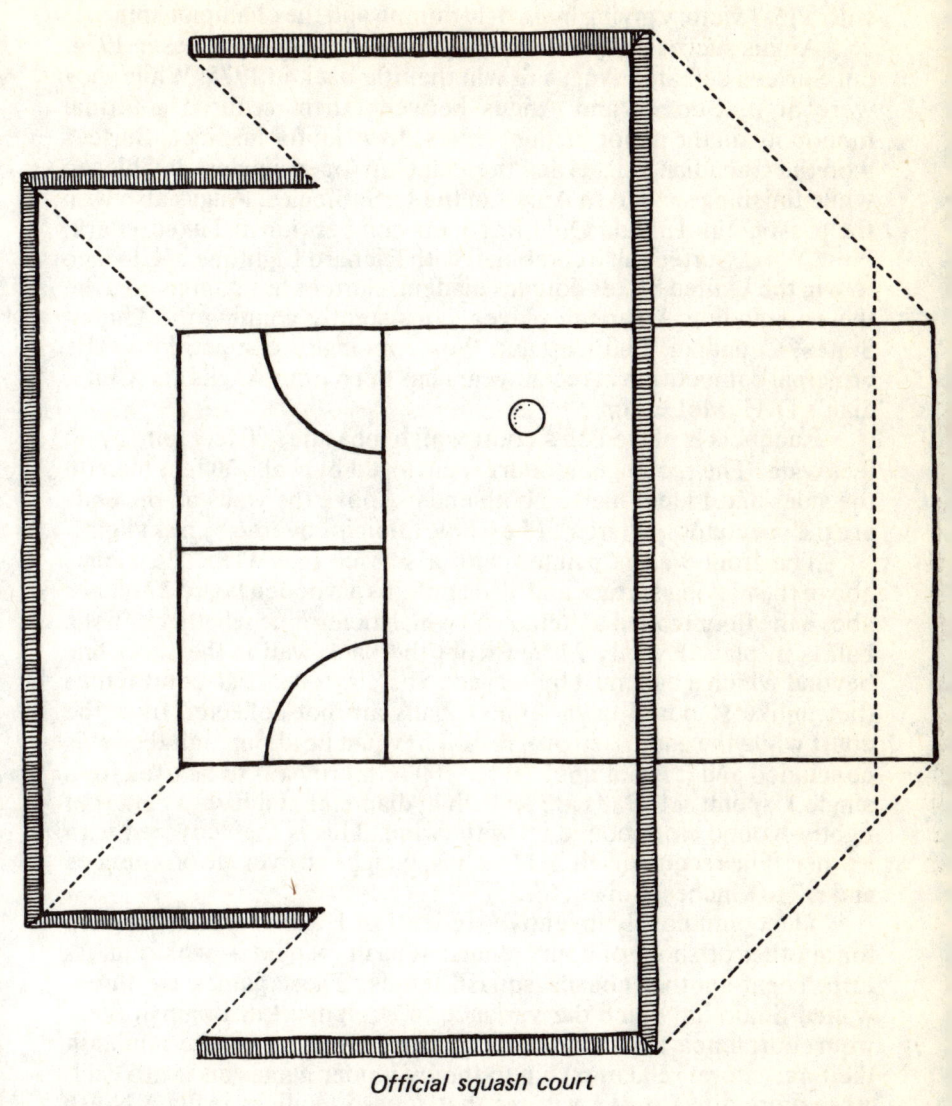
Official squash court showing walls

set at London on March 24, 15-9, but then Angus closed out the series with a 15-3 victory giving him a 5-1 triumph and the championship.

Angus successfully defended the crown against Surtees in 1974, but Surtees defeated Angus to win the title back in 1975. While they were at it, Surtees and Angus between them secured a virtual monopoly on the major racquets titles. In 1973, for instance, Surtees won the Canadian singles and the Pell Cup (open singles) at Chicago while finishing second to Angus in the U.S. Singles. Angus also won the prestigious Tuxedo Gold Racquets competition at Tuxedo Park, New York. Surtees also combined with Richard Lightfine of Chicago to win the United States doubles diadem. Surtees has continued to be the outstanding American player, consistently winning the United States, Canadian, Pell Cup and Western singles competitions. His principal competition in recent years has been from Angus and Canadian's D.H. McLernon.

Racquets is played on a court which measures 60 feet long by 30 feet wide. The rectangular court is enclosed by walls 30 feet high on the sides and 15 feet high on both ends. Above the walls on the ends are the spectators galleries. The whole affair is covered by a skylight.

The front wall is painted with a service line 9 feet 7½ inches above the playing surface and also contains a wooden board 27 inches above the floor (called a "telltale") which determine whether or not a ball is in play. Exactly 24 feet from the back wall is the short line beyond which a ball must be served to be playable. Like court tennis (but unlike standard lawn tennis), balls are not collected from the court while the game is in progress. They just lie about until the set is concluded and it is not unusual for 100 or more balls to be used for a single 15-point set. Balls are an inch in diameter and have a center of tightly-wound cloth bound up with twine. This is then covered with leather. The racquet itself is 30 inches, weighs an average of 9 ounces and is 7 to 8 inches in diameter.

The continuously inventive students of Harrow are responsible for another offshoot of court tennis: squash racquets—which, in its turn, begat another cousin, squash tennis. These games are three-walled affairs in which the variance in equipment distinguish them from court tennis and racquets. But the games generally are similar in their ancestoral relalationship to the two older games and with each other more directly. We will see that squash tennis is really a North American variant of the British squash racquets.

About 1850, the Harrow boys sought to create a game which had the attributes of racquets with none of the drawbacks caused by the

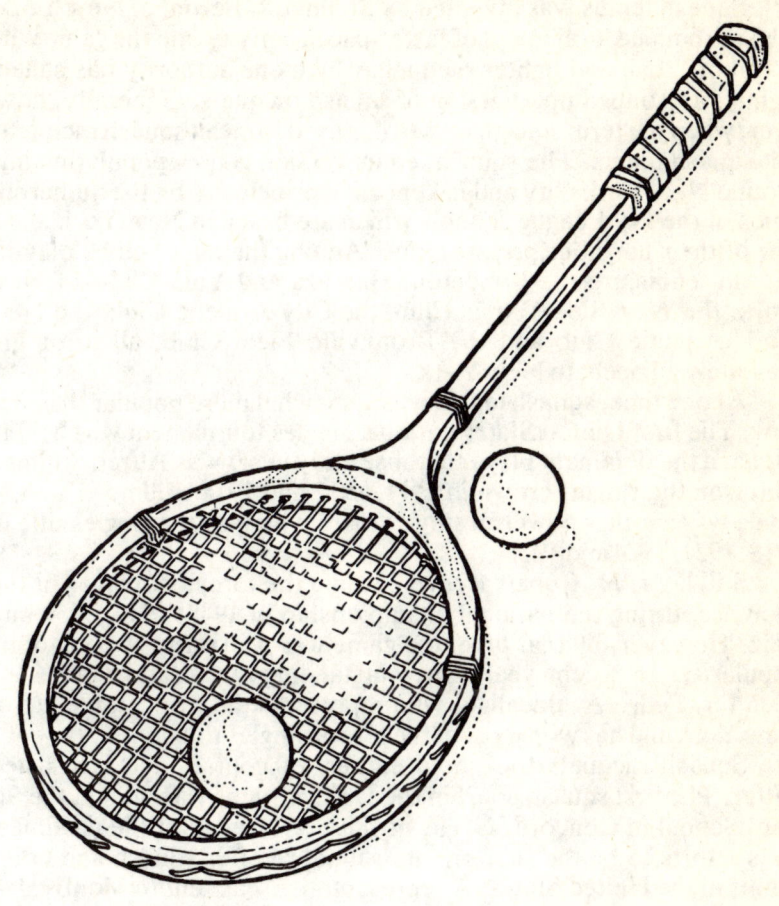

Standard squash racquet

large size of the court and the liveliness of the ball. What they invented was squash or squash racquets. Its chief competition is squash tennis.

Squash tennis was invented by Stephen J. Feron, of New York, who introduced an element of faster-paced activity into the game with a "rabbit" ball and lighter racquets which one authority has called, rightly, a "souped up" version of squash racquets. Generally, however, when the term squash is used it is used to mean squash racquets, not squash tennis. The squash tennis version is now popular mainly around New York City and is kept alive principally by the numerous clubs of the Ivy League schools which are based in New York and a few of their neighbor private clubs. Among the major clubs playing squash tennis are the Princeton, Harvard and Yale Clubs of New York, the West Side Tennis Club, the City Athletic Club, the New York Athletic Club and the Bronxville Field Club, all in or immediately adjacent to New York.

At one time, squash tennis was somewhat more popular than it is now. The first United States national singles tournament was held in 1911 and the dominant player in those early years was Alfred Stillman who won the singles crown in 1911, 1912 and 1914. Fillmore Van S. Hyde was another powerful singles man, who won the singles title in 1918, 1921, 1924 and 1926.

Still later, H. Robert Reeve became the foremost player of the sport, capturing the national championship in 1948, 1949, 1950 and 1952. However, by that time, the game was well past the peak of its popularity. In recent years, the outstanding man in this game has been Dr. Pedro A. Bacallao, who represents the Princeton Club of New York and has won most of the recent singles titles.

Squash racquets took hold earlier, of course, and has lasted better. The first squash court in the United States was built at the St. Paul School in Concord, N.H., in 1882, as a result of the headmaster's efforts to be the first private school to offer squash and court tennis in the United States. A representative was sent to Montreal to learn the games and get the dimensions for the courts.

But the first real advance in popularity for squash racquets in America came in 1893 with the opening of The Racquets Club in Philadelphia. It was then that squash began to take on some semblance of popular appeal. By 1907, championship tournaments were being held. But it was this burst of enthusiasm for squash racquets that brought on the birth of the Americanized squash tennis and sidetracked squash racquets for awhile. In 1898, the fabled Tuxedo Club in Tuxedo Park, New York, built a court and elected to use it for squash tennis, feeling it more "American". The National Squash Tennis Association was formed in 1911 and the following year formal competition was begun in New York with Stillman as the defending champion in the singles event.

However, squash racquets was able to hold its own and it had one advantage that squash tennis never really achieved—it was international in scope. It was this fact, probably more than any other, which enabled it to survive and thrive as much as it has.

The Lapham Cup, pitting the best fifteen men in the United States and Canada against each other in singles matches, was started in 1922 and continues to the present. The Canadian team is very competitive with the United States and won as recently as 1973 by the score of 8 matches to 7. The United States routed the Canadian team in 1975, 11 matches to 4, and has a lead in the series. Another example of the international aspect of squash racquets is the Wolfe-Noel Challenge Matches which sets women's teams from the United States and England against each other in an annual series begun in 1933. Among its major boosters was the Duke of Windsor, the former Edward VII of Great Britain, who, before his death in 1970, was a major supporter of squash racquets and did much to further competition in the game, especially between the United States and England.

Oddly enough, the first United States Open championship in squash racquets wasn't staged until 1954 at the University Club in New York.

The most consistent champion, since the inauguration of the competition for the singles' crown, has been Vic Neiderhoffer, of Brooklyn, who won his first title in 1966, displacing Stephen T. Vehslage of New York. The Open title has been dominated in recent years by two men.

Mohibulla Kahn, of Boston, was the dominant player in the early 1960's, before Ralph E. Howe of New York won the Open in 1967. Howe, himself, was a former United States National singles champion in 1964. But Mohibulla Kahn again won the Open in 1968. Then another Kahn, this one from Canada, took the Open in 1969 and held the crown for six successive years until Neiderhoffer finally broke his streak in 1975.

The Harvard-educated Neiderhoffer had been the national intercollegiate champion in 1964. Harvard has generally dominated the intercollegiate competition with Anil Nayar winning the college event in 1967, 1968 and 1969, Lawrence Terrell in 1970 and Peter Briggs in 1972 and 1973.

The squash games are played on a court which, for singles, is 18½ feet wide, 32 feet long and 16 feet high at the front wall. The ball must strike the front wall at least 17 inches above the playing floor, a line at that height being indicated by the squash version of the "telltale", a metal strip running across the frontwall.

Serves must hit above a line across the frontwall 6½ feet off the floor, the "frontwall service line" which is drawn on the wall. There is also a "floor service line" 22 feet from and parallel with, the front wall. The player serves from a designated area behind this line. Still another line divides the court into equal portions at right angles to the front wall. This line designates the service courts. A served ball must hit the front wall above the service line and bound into the opposite service court. The ball must be returned by the opponent before it bounces twice or lose the point.

The man winning the point also earns (or retains) the right to serve again and continue scoring. Like handball, only the server can score. Generally, games are played until one man reaches 15 points. However, if, in any game, the score becomes tied at 13 points, the man to first reach 13 can peg the winning total (or "set" as it is called) at either 15, 16 or 18 and the game is then played to the point which he has selected and the first man to hit that figure is the winner.

The squash racquet ball is composed of hard rubber and has very little bounce. The racquet is very similar to a badminton racquet which is, itself, a reduced-scale version of the tennis racquet.

The mention of badminton brings us to an interesting point: badminton is not related in any way to the racquet games of the tennis family, a common misconception. Badminton is an Eastern game which was very popular in India during the early years of the British suzerainty and was brought to England by returning colonials. The game, originally known in India as *poona* was introduced to England by the Duke of Beaufort at his palatial country estate which was called Badminton. "The Badminton Game" was first played in Britain in 1873 and became very popular there. Competitions were organized shortly thereafter. The All-England championship is still one of the major events of the badminton world, but the game remains strongest in the India subcontinent where most of the best players are produced.

The countries of Malaya, Indonesia, Ceylon (Sri Lanka) and India have consistently developed the strongest badminton clubs throughout this century and in the West, only Denmark has come close to matching their output of good players and teams, although

The court

the United States has developed one outstanding female player, Judy Devlin Hashman of Baltimore. As Miss Devlin and, later, Mrs. Hashman, she won the All-England women's title 10 times between 1954 and 1967.

But we digress.

The squash racquets racquet bears a resemblance to the one used in badminton except that it has a longer handle and is somewhat heavier and sturdier.

Squash tennis differs in that the ball has a resemblance to the lawn tennis ball with its fast-action and high bouncing qualities. The racquet used in squash tennis is also much like the tennis racquet in use throughout the world today, except that the handle is about an inch or so shorter.

It must also be observed that there are some differences in equipment and playing style between squash racquets played in North America and that played in international competition elsewhere in the world, chiefly in countries that are now in the British Commonwealth or part of the former British Empire. The major difference is that the international ball is a bit softer and plays slower, which reduces the amount of backwall play and cuts down on the chances for a recovery. As a result, points in international competition tend to be longer, although less spectacular, than those in North America.

In international play, the racquet is about 2 ounces lighter than the United States and Canadian ones and the court is 2½ feet wider with uniformly natural wood floors rather than the artificial surfaces common in North America. In recent years, Australia has dominated international competition, frequently winning the world team title with a team built around a great star, Cam Nancarrow. Other countries which regularly compete in the world competition are Great Britain, South Africa, New Zealand and Canada, as well as the United States. The American team is not involved in this class of competition on a regular basis.

The international style, it may be observed, puts great stress on stamina since the ball must always be played quickly rather than on caroms and rebounds. Also, most of the international stars are devoted first to the game and then, very secondarily, to their means of livelihood, whatever it may be. This, of course, is not the case in the United States and Canada. Several Australian and New Zealand professionals have emigrated to Canada and the United States in recent years and have dominated competitions which they have entered. The world team tournament is usually held every two years in odd-numbered years.

Now we come to the most popular outgrowth of court tennis: lawn tennis or, as it is known in North America and as I shall refer to it hereafter, tennis. The development, in Germany, of a ball which could be used out of doors was the beginning of the craze of tennis as we know it today.

The court tennis ball is similar to the baseball. It is encased in a stitched cover and is filled with baseball-like materials such as twine, thread, cloth and hair without the cork center. It has little bouncing power, especially on grass or natural turf. But the invention by Charles Goodyear of vulcanization and the refinement by the Germans of a light, thinly-walled rubber ball made outdoor tennis a possibility. The ball did not need a hard surface to make it bounce.

That possibility was brought to reality by Walter Clopton Wingfield, in England. On a warm December day in 1873, he introduced a new game to a lawn party of his friends at Nantclwyd and the following February filed for a patent for the rules and playing court which was subsequently issued on July 24, 1874. In the meantime, Wingfield had published his book of rules for the game and tennis was on its way. He originally called his game "Sphairistike" which his friends shortened to "sticky." But the name has vanished from the lexicon but the game remains very much with us.

Wingfield, however, was not long involved in the course of affairs. The Marylebone Cricket Club, the world's authority on that game, had taken an active role in codifying the rules of court tennis and offered to take the same position with respect to the new game when a series of disputes broke out over Wingfield's rules and court design, including challenges to his patents. Wingfield, gracefully, bowed out and the M.C.C. appointed an all-star committee of sportsmen to step in and organize the game. They did.

But the Marylebone, with its very high-tone membership, was not long to rule the tennis roost. In 1875, the All-England Croquet Club invited tennis and badminton players to join their club. Within two years, tennis was far and away the dominant sport at the All-England Croquet Club and its name was added to the title of the club. In 1877, the club staged its first championship tournament, which was won by Spencer Gore, who, incidentally, was an accomplished racquets man. The event was such a success that it has been staged annually ever since and is now concluding its first century.

But the tournament is popularly known by the name of the town where the club is located: Wimbledon.

The All-England, or Wimbledon, remains to this day probably the most prestigious of all tennis events with the United States Open at Forest Hills, New York, certainly a very close second by any standard. The French and Austrialian championships are the other events which make up the so-called "Big Four" of the Grand Slam of tennis.

In 1881, the game has become sufficiently established in America for the first national association to be formed: the United States National Lawn Tennis Association, now shortened to the United States Tennis Association, or U.S.T.A. Seven years later, a second national association was formed, this time in England: the Lawn Tennis Association, or L.T.A. Subsequently, the International Lawn Tennis Federation was created to embrace all of the national organizations. However, rivalry between Wimbledon (which was in) and Forest Hills (which wasn't) kept the United States out of the I.L.T.F. until 1923.

There has been a considerable dispute over the years about how tennis was introduced into the United States. Some say Mary Outerbridge first played it on Staten Island in 1874. Others claim two New England gentlemen introduced it at Nahant, a summer resort outside of Boston, in 1874 as well. Miss Outerbridge was a member of an influential Staten Island family and took her tennis racquet in hand at the Staten Island Cricket and Baseball Club in St. George. This club, incidentally, has a long and interesting history. At one time it served as the home field of a major league baseball team in the 1880's: the original New York Mets who won the American Association pennant in 1884 and played in the first official World Series against Providence of the National League that October. The club is also the seedbed of cricket in the U.S. and its present day members play the old English game at Walker Park to this day.

In spite of the formidable arguments on behalf of Mary Outerbridge, equally impressive points can be made for Dr. James Dwight and Richard Sears, the two gentlemen of Nahant, Massachusetts.

Regardless of who is responsible for its introduction, tennis rapidly became an extremely popular game in America and, in 1881, under the auspices of the U.S.N.L.T.A., a national singles championship was staged at the Newport Casino in Rhode Island. The tournament was won by the aforementioned Richard Sears who defeated W.E. Glyn 6-0, 6-3, 6-2. Sears reigned as the U.S. champion until 1888 when H.W. Slocum, Jr., won the crown.

Sears was able to hold the title for seven years partly because the tournament was conducted on a challenge-round basis, in which the defending champion waits until all competitors have played each other and then faces the winner for the final match. This system, clearly, gives some advantage to the defending champion. However, it wasn't until 1912 that the challenge-round was abolished and no one ever seriously questioned Sears' seven successive singles titles.

In 1915, after 34 years, the tournament was moved from Newport to the slightly less exclusive West Side Tennis Club in Forest Hills, New York, where it has remained (except for 1921-23) and where it has grown into the largest annual international tennis competition.

In the 1920's, tennis boomed as a spectator sport as well as a recreational game, and it had the perfect spur—a genuine superstar. Big Bill Tilden was to tennis in the 1920's what Babe Ruth was to baseball during the same era. A headline name, the star of the game and a big box office attraction. From 1920 to 1925, he won six straight U.S. titles at Forest Hills and the Germantown Cricket Club, in Philadelphia, and also lead the Davis Cup team for the United States. America won the Davis Cup seven years running (1920-1926) with Tilden and many of the matches were played before capacity crowds at Forest Hills and Germantown where he was also winning United States annual championships. An illustration of the growth of tennis can be seen in the increase in the number of countries competing for the Davis Cup.

Not only were the crowds larger, but the fields were steadily growing in the international competition. It was during these years that the Davis Cup became a major international sports event, grabbing a big share of newspaper space and pulling fans through the turnstiles. In 1920, when the U.S. defeated a combination of Australia and New Zealand (called Australsia), only five countries entered the challenging competition. By 1928, when France beat the U.S. for the Cup, 4-1, at Paris, 33 nations had entered the challenge competition.

Tilden ultimately turned professional which, at that time, disqualified him from competing for the U.S. National singles at Forest Hills or playing on the Davis Cup team. He was succeeded by generations of outstanding American players including Ellsworth

Vines, Fred Perry, Don Budge, Bobby Riggs, Frank Parker, Richard (Pancho) Gonzales, Vic Seixas, Arthur Ashe, Stan Smith and Jimmy Connors, among others.

Tennis became a huge North American industry and a worldwide sport. Today it is still the fastest-growing sport internationally.

However, it may shortly have competition for the North American recreational attention (and the spectator dollars) from a rather new creation, racquetball, which is still a further outgrowth of paddleball, another distant cousin of court tennis.

Paddleball is rather a combination of handball (a game more-or-less born and bred in Ireland where it is still extremely popular) and court tennis concepts.

While paddleball, an invention of the 1930's, appears to be on the decline in its original four-wall version, a one-walled version, popular in the eastern areas, remains very popular. And racquetball, highly successful on the West Coast, appears to be gaining in popularity which may soon make it a major North American sport for both recreation and spectator interest.

They must, then, be added to the long list of games which have already sprung from the original court tennis, indeed a fascinating game, even if judged solely by its offspring.

chapter 2

Court Tennis

COURT TENNIS, a virtually non-existent participation sport, is included in this book because of its fascinating history and its function as the "father of games" which include, not necessarily in order of prominence, tennis, platform tennis, racquets, squash racquets and squash tennis, racquetball, deck tennis, volleyball, fronton tennis, jai-alai, paddleball, paddle tennis, pelota, table tennis, and net tennis, among others.

But it also has a fairly long and colorful history, having marked its first century of play in the United States. The game of real, royal or court tennis was introduced into the United States in the American Revolution Centennial Year of 1876. It was in Boston, the seedbed of the revolution against Britain, that the game was introduced from that very same country.

Hollis Hunnewell and Nathaniel Thayer constructed a court tennis court in Boston in 1876 and engaged Ted Hunt, an English professional, as the resident teacher and keeper of the court. It is interesting to note that by whatever accounts you may accept, lawn tennis (or, in North America, tennis) was introduced to this country at least two years before its ancient ancestor made the voyage across the Atlantic. This despite the disparity in ages between the two games themselves.

But once it was established here, court tennis spread rather rapidly, especially considering the costs involved.

The wonderfully-archaic old court which is faithfully reproduced wherever the game is played is a large part of the fascination (for the viewer), the aggravation (for the player) and the expense (for the builder) of court tennis. Because of its size and expense, construction of courts has steadily reduced to a mere handful today in England and France.

America, without the huge backlog of existing courts from which to start, never has had a substantial number of them. But after the construction of the first by Hunnewell and Thayer in Boston, the Newport Casino followed suit in 1880 and the Boston Athletic Association did as well in 1888. Shortly thereafter, courts came to New York and Philadelphia and, finally, there was a basis for national competition in the U.S.

One of the events which spurred the growth of the game in North America was the presence of Tom Pettitt. He had come as a frightened, 12 year-old, immigrant boy from England in 1876 to serve as an assistant to Hunt at the original Boston court. He had shown some promise and a good deal of interest in the game in his native land and the move to Boston, even though it placed the boy on foreign shores, was thought to be an excellent opportunity for him to improve his lot in life. So did it prove to be.

In less than a decade the now-fully-grown Pettitt was one of the world's great masters of the game and, in 1885, he became the first internationally recognized champion that court tennis had ever had in its long and colorful history.

Court tennis may be the only game in which America spawned a world champion before it had a national champion of its own. The first United States national singles competition wasn't held until 1892, when Pettitt had already reigned as the world titlist for seven years. His exploits naturally aided the growth of interest in the game.

At that initial 1892 United States court tennis tournament, a unique thing happened. Richard D. Sears, who was the first U.S.N.L.T.A. tennis singles champion and who won the title for the next 6 years as well, had taken a fancy to court tennis—the regal ancestor of the game he dominated. Sears had used the Newport Casino court to full advantage and in 1892, he became the United States champion of court tennis, too. He was the only sportsman ever to be the first winner of two separate national championship tournaments.

However, he reigned only briefly as king of court tennis. In 1893, Fiske Warren succeeded him to the title and the next two years, B. Spalding de Garmendia was the U.S. titleholder. Lawrence M. Stockton, one of the top early players in the country, captured three of the next four crowns (1896, 1898 and 1899) with George R. Fearing, Jr., taking the other in 1897. The first foreign winner in the tournament was Eustace Miles, of England, in 1900. Among other Britishers to win the U.S. tournament have been George Huband, in 1927, and Lord Aberdare, in 1930. Joshua Crane was the champion from 1901 to 1904 and then Charles E. Sands won in 1905.

Although Pettitt never competed for the United States national championship the fact remains he was a world champion. The next world champion produced in America was to hold the crown for nineteen years. Jay Gould, world court tennis king from 1914 to 1916, won his first U.S. title in 1906, defended it successfully through 1917 when World War I interrupted competition for two years and then retained the championship in competition from 1920 to 1925. He was never beaten in a singles match in championship play.

Finally, C. Suyden Cutting took over in 1926, Huband in 1927 and Hewitt Morgan in 1928-1929. After Lord Aberdare's win in 1930, William C. Wright won two straight titles and James H. Van Alen, part of a famous family of racquets and tennis players, was the champion in 1933.

Another of the famous names which grace the history of the game in America, Ogden Phipps of horse racing fame, was the holder of the title for four years until 1937. Alastair B. Martin won in 1940. Both Phipps (three times) and Martin (twice) were later to challenge the great Pierre Etchebaster for the world title, but without success.

World War II again suspended competition until 1946, when Robert Grant, 3rd, became the champion. But the era was really that of Northrup B. Knox, the next American to win the world title. Upon Etchebaster's ultimate retirement in 1954, Knox was coming into his own. E.M. Beals, Jr., had won the U.S. title in 1947, being displaced by Phipps in 1948 and 1949, and Martin in 1950 through 1952. But Knox was the next dominant American in the game and after two Englishmen, James Dear and Albert B. Johnson traded the title back and forth, Knox beat Johnson in 1959.

After his victory over Johnson, 7 sets to 2, Knox made only two challenge defenses of his title in the next nine years, successfully turning back both challenges without difficulty and establishing himself as one of the greats in the last century of the game perhaps on a par with Pettitt, Gould and Etchebaster.

In 1966, Knox faced Ronald Hughes, of Great Britain, in New York on February 8 and 10, following the ancient tradition of taking a break between groups of sets in a challenge match. On the court of the Racquet and Tennis Club, Knox won the first four sets on February 8, 6-0, 6-3, 6-5 and 6-0. The outcome was already clear. Knox completed his sweep of the best 7-of-13 with three more wins on February 10, 6-1, 6-1, 6-3, dropping a total of only 13 points while winning 42 and completing the first sweep (7-0 in sets) of a challenge championship since Etchebaster beat Martin in 1950. It also marked the only third such sweep in the competition since the days of Tom Pettitt. Even Gould, perhaps the finest American-born player in the history of the game, was never able to shutout a world class opponent in a challenge series.

Meanwhile, the American game had fallen into the hands of the Bostwick brothers, George H. (Pete) and James F.C., famous sportsmen well-known for their exploits in many sports since the 1950's. In 1964, the U.S. amateur was an all-Bostwick affair with Jimmy beating Pete, 4-6, 6-2, 6-4, 2-6, 7-5, at New York. That same year, incidentally, Britisher Ronald Hughes, won the U.S. open singles.

In 1966, Pete Bostwick won the amateur and the open, defeating New York professional Joe O'Donnell for the open crown, 6-2, 6-4, 6-1, at Tuxedo Park. The next year, Jimmy beat Pete for the open championship at New York but Pete beat Luis Dominguez, 6-1, 6-2, 6-1, for the amateur title. In 1968, at Philadelphia, Pete won his fourth straight U.S. amateur by downing James L. Van Alen, 2nd, 6-1, 3-6, 6-5, 6-1, on his own home court.

Pete Bostwick then felt ready for a challenge to Knox. It wasn't the wisest thought ever to enter his mind. However, Bostwick gave a slightly better account of himself against the almost impregnable Knox than Bostwick. The series opened in New York on February 10 with Knox taking a 3-set-to-1 edge on scores of 6-5, 2-6, 6-3, and 6-3. On February 12, Bostwick won the first set, 6-2, but lost the next three, 6-3, 6-4, and 6-4, to trail by a total of 6 to 2. It was obvious that Knox was going to easily defend his title, but custom dictated that no more than four sets be played on any given day so the denouement was held over to February 14 when the stubborn Bostwick won again, 6-2, but lost the tenth set, 6-5, and Knox emerged with a 7-3 triumph.

Since the Bostwicks were the measure of the best that the world then had to offer, Knox retired from competition after that victory. With the competition then opened to all legitimate comers, Pete Bostwick, as the last challenger to the retired champion, accepted a challenge from England's Frank Willis and the two contested for the vacant throne in 1969 with Bostwick winning, 11 sets 8.

The next two challenges were totally Bostwick family events with Pete and Jimmy facing each other in 1970 and 1972. In 1970, Pete defended his crown with a 7-set-to-2 victory, but in 1972, Jimmy unseated him with a reversal by exactly the same score.

Jimmy Bostwick accepted and turned back a challenge from racquets champion Howard R. Angus of England, 7-sets-to-5, in 1974, keeping America's control of the world court tennis title at a string of 15 years.

Meanwhile, a new star arose on the horizon of court tennis in

America. Eugene Scott, a New York attorney, became a serious threat in 1973 when he lost in the semifinals to Pete Bostwick, the recently-dethroned world titlist, in five sets. Gene Scott, a one-time standout amateur tennis player who was ranked in the top ten among Eastern players in the U.S., won the first set, 6-3, and took the third, amazingly, 6-0, forcing Bostwick to rally when trailing in sets, 2-1, to advance to the finals against Angus. Scott that year won the U.S. Open and the prestigious Tuxedo Gold Racquet competitions. By 1975, he was the dominant player in the game, sweeping all of the major U.S. events, beating Pete Bostwick in straight sets for the amateur title and turning back another newcomer, Ralph E. Howe of New York, in both the Tuxedo Gold Racquet and United States Open, winning six of seven sets from Howe in the process.

In 1975, this new rising star, in fact, reached the top. Jimmy Bostwick retired from international competition which, again, vacated the title and opened it up for challenge on both sides of the Atlantic. Scott was the American selected to defend the title for the U.S. and he accepted a challenge from Britain's Howard Angus. The competition opened at the Racquet and Tennis Club on March 29 and 31, and was completed at the Queen's Club in London on April 11. Scott defeated Angus and became the fourth successive American to hold the title since it was won by Northrup Knox in 1959.

Scott remained active in 1976 even though there was no international challenge for his world title. He successfully defended his championships in the Tuxedo Gold Racquet where he defeated Howe in an uncharacteristically sloppy match in which neither man was outstanding and in the United States amateur and open singles. In the open, which as its name impies is open to competitors from any nation, he defeated touring professional Barry Toates of Tasmania, 3 sets to 1.

Aside from the matches played at Tuxedo Park and New York's Racquet and Tennis Club, other active courts include those at Boston and Philadelphia. A privately-owned court exists at Aiken, South Carolina, where both the Knox and Bostwick families are active in its maintainence. Another exists at Lakewood, New Jersey, at the former country estate of Jay Gould. However, a girls' college now occupies the buildings and this court is only little used. The court which once graced the Chicago Racquet Club was torn out some years ago.

However, there seems to be something of a resurgence of interest in this ancient game. In recent years, two new courts have been constructed in Melbourne, Australia, and a move is afoot to build at least one, and perhaps two more, in Sydney. There has also been considerable movement toward the construction of additional courts in New York and other parts of North America.

As has been previously mentioned, it is the court itself which lends much of the mystery and charm to this oldest of racquet games.

There have been many explanations as to why the court is constructed with all of its peculiarities. But one must bear in mind that the game reached the height of its popularity, among all of the classes of the structured societies in England and France in the 16th and 17th centuries. Feudalism was on the wane, but hardly vanished when the game was evolving. The most logical explanation for why many of the unusual items are included in the court construction is that each of them relate to a particular segment of the society which was prevalent during the formative years of the court.

While it can be dangerous to over estimate the number of people who played the game in Europe during its peak decades, it is clear that men from all walks of life were active in it and it was the dominant indoor athletic exercise, perhaps to the exclusion of all others in many cases. During the time when court tennis was developing, it was found more desirable to alter the primary game than split it off into many secondary games.

For instance, racquetball is a spinoff of paddleball, designed by those who found the latter game too slow for their energies. Paddleball, itself, is a child of handball, conjured up by those who didn't wish to subject their hands to the brutal pounding administered by the constant contact with a rock-hard ball.

Court tennis, rather than breed subsidiary games, incorporated many different ideas into its own game. Later, it ultimately became the source of many subsidiary games which were extractions of some of these elements expressed independently. Almost all court and racquet-style games include either walls, nets to hit the ball over, or floor markings for targets. Court tennis embodies all of them.

When the game, with its extraordinary court, was first introduced to North America is a matter of speculation. Some authorities have cited references to courts in New York in the pre-revolutionary days and the famous Tory editor James Rivington is supposed to have imported implements for its playing in 1766. But one tends to doubt that a full-scale court was constructed in the United States at that time. The first documented construction of a court was the one in Boston in 1876 at the present site of Back Bay Station.

The oldest active court in existence in the United States is the famous one at the Tuxedo Club in Tuxedo Park, New York, which was opened for play in 1900.

It is likely that the game itself was played in some truncated versions here long before the revolution and certainly was well known here prior to the construction of the 1876 Boston court. But without the court in its full detail, the game loses much of its interest. One of the colonial sources often quoted on this subject was a proclamation by Gov. Peter Stuyvesant of New York (Nieu Amsterdam) of Sept. 30, 1659, which "interdict and forbid" the playing of several games including tennis, all offshoots of court tennis.

Some of the more famous patrons of the game who built courts privately over the years in America included Gould (whose court, as we have mentioned, still exists), Payne Whitney and Clarence Mackey.

When the game was introduced, or reintroduced, to New York in 1891 by the Racquet and Tennis Club, it resulted in the building of the Chicago Racquet Club court in 1893, in conjunction with the Columbia Exposition there, but both of these original courts have been torn down.

Racquets weigh about a pound and are normally 27 inches or so long. The balls are slightly smaller than today's tennis variety. The racquet heads are shaped with an inclination toward one side to allow for chopping cuts of the ball on the service and are strung with heavy gut.

Since this involves all of the variation probably possible in a court-and-racquet game, there are several ways of winning a point. But the thing which makes court tennis really unique is the chase lines. The chase is what prevents the game from being a hitter's game and makes it a game of finesse above all. Matches are called by a "marker" who has, as one of his major functions, calling the chases when the ball hits the floor.

It is not probable that even the best explanation of the game can give a clear picture of court tennis without having first seen it, but, in general, the way the game is played as follows.

A ball hit into the grille, dedans or the so-called "winning gallery" at the hazard end is a point won. But these are tough targets and the chase is the more important element. When one man makes a shot, and, the other player cannot return the ball before it hits the floor for a second time, the marker calls a chase, let's say, "last gallery."

There exists in this game the possibility of changing sides during the course of playing a point, rather than at the end of series of points, as is usual in other games. For instance, if the marker calls "chase a yard" on a ball which strikes the floor less than a yard from the end wall of the service end, the two players change sides. In fact, the only time they will change sides is to play off a chase call.

After the change of sides, the man who failed to play the ball originally must keep his shots, during the ensuing rally, deep enough to hit the floor on its second bound within a yard of the wall or within the confines of the chase called. The man who struck the shot originally keeps returning the ball until his opponent hits a shot that is further out than the chase called. He lets it go and wins the point.

Of course, during the playing of a rally, a point can always be won by an error such as the ball going into the net or a ball that hits above certain markings on the walls.

With respect to service, there are an almost infinite variety, including some with such colorful names as drop, giraffe, pound, sidewall and underhand twist. Serves must be hit onto the penthouse roof before they are in play and the ball often rolls along the roof for awhile before dropping onto the floor where it can be played—perhaps.

Allison Danzig, a very skillful and knowledgeable court tennis writer and native of America, is fond of this description of the game: "it has been described as a game of moving chess, combining the exactitude of billiards, the coordination of hand and eye of lawn tennis and the generalship, and the quick judgement of polo." That puts the case well, although it may err on the side of understatement.

In 1767, a French authority said, "It is the only game which can take rank in the list of arts . . ."

Court tennis puts a premium on judgment, stamina, patience and skill rather than sheer strength or speed. Accuracy matters most.

chapter 3

Racquetball

RACQUETBALL IS FAIRLY NEW, as games go, but it has already developed a fascinating and colorful history, replete with hereos and villians.

The sport is also one which, in keeping with the times in North America, has turned into a professional game probably in a shorter period than any other sport in history. For example, take a look at other popular North American sports. Baseball was standardized by Alexander Cartwright in 1845 and the first professional league didn't start play until 1871, 26 years later. Football saw its first collegiate game in 1869 and its first pro encounter in 1895, a span of 26 years as well. Basketball was invented in 1891 and within 10 years was being played as a pro sport, but didn't develop into a national league status until 1946.

Our friend racquetball, on the other hand, saw its first national amateur competition in 1969 in St. Louis, and began its first professional circuit only four years later, in 1973.

But to be perfectly honest, racquetball had a long history of development which led up to that first national competition in 1969 and paddleball (which will be discussed in detail in a later chapter) must be considered as part of that history since it is an offshoot of court tennis as well. In fact, racquetball may be threatening the four-wall version of paddleball with extinction.

A man from Greenwich, Connecticut, Joe Sobek, is generally acknowledged as the "Father of Racquetball." In 1950, Sobek left his work as a squash and tennis instructor for a desk job. In search of recreation for himself, strolled into the Greenwich Y.M.C.A. where he discarded the idea of handball as being too hard on his hands and took up paddleball. He soon came to the conclusion, as a squash and tennis man, that paddleball played with a racquet would be a much more interesting game than plain paddleball, because of the resiliency of the stringed racquet. He was right, but his theory didn't prove itself out immediately.

He ordered custom-made racquets (25 total) and began to introduce his friends to the game. It was immediately popular but ran into a snag when the supply of balls then being used was exhausted. It developed that those balls had been part of an old order which had lain about the shelves of the Y.M.C.A. for an appreciable length of time. It took a while for Sobek to locate a supplier for that particular kind of ball. When he finally found a manufacturer, he was forced to order 150 dozen, the minimum amount.

"Unfortunately," said Sobek later, "I was stuck with those balls since they were too lively and completely unsuitable for play. I figured I would have to wait two years before the balls went flat and were the same as the old ones we had been using.

"During this waiting period, I approached one of the country's most reputable rubber ball manufacturers and they agreed to try to meet my rigid specs.

"After much time and expense, the present official ball resulted.

"With a fine quality racquet and ball, paddle racquets (now racquetball) became a sensation in Greenwich. As people left Greenwich for other cities, they introduced the game to their new 'Y' and the next thing I knew, there would be a request for equipment."

Slowly over the years, the word spread across the country and, along the way, struck up hot sparks in certain areas. The game, for instance, became a sensation in St. Louis, where even now the local 'Y' is one of the premiere spawning grounds for racquetball players and has produced many of the top stars in the game. It has also become a very hot item in San Diego, California, largely through the efforts of a dentist, Dr. Bud Muehleisen. Muehleisen was a longtime nationally-ranked paddleball star and twice national paddleball singles champion. Muehleisen's conversion to racquetball took place in the late 1960's and inspired a number of his proteges to switch, too.

Muehleisen also became the first national racquetball singles champion by virtue of winning that 1969 tournament. He relates an interesting story about how the tournament was planned without a title because the game itself had no formal name. Joe Sobek had called it paddle racquets which sounds like a game played by mobsters. The promoters sought to find something more descriptive.

Muehleisen says, "Finally, Bob McInerny (a San Diego tennis teacher) came up with 'racquetball'. So there you have it: a 25 year-old sport with a 5 year-old name."

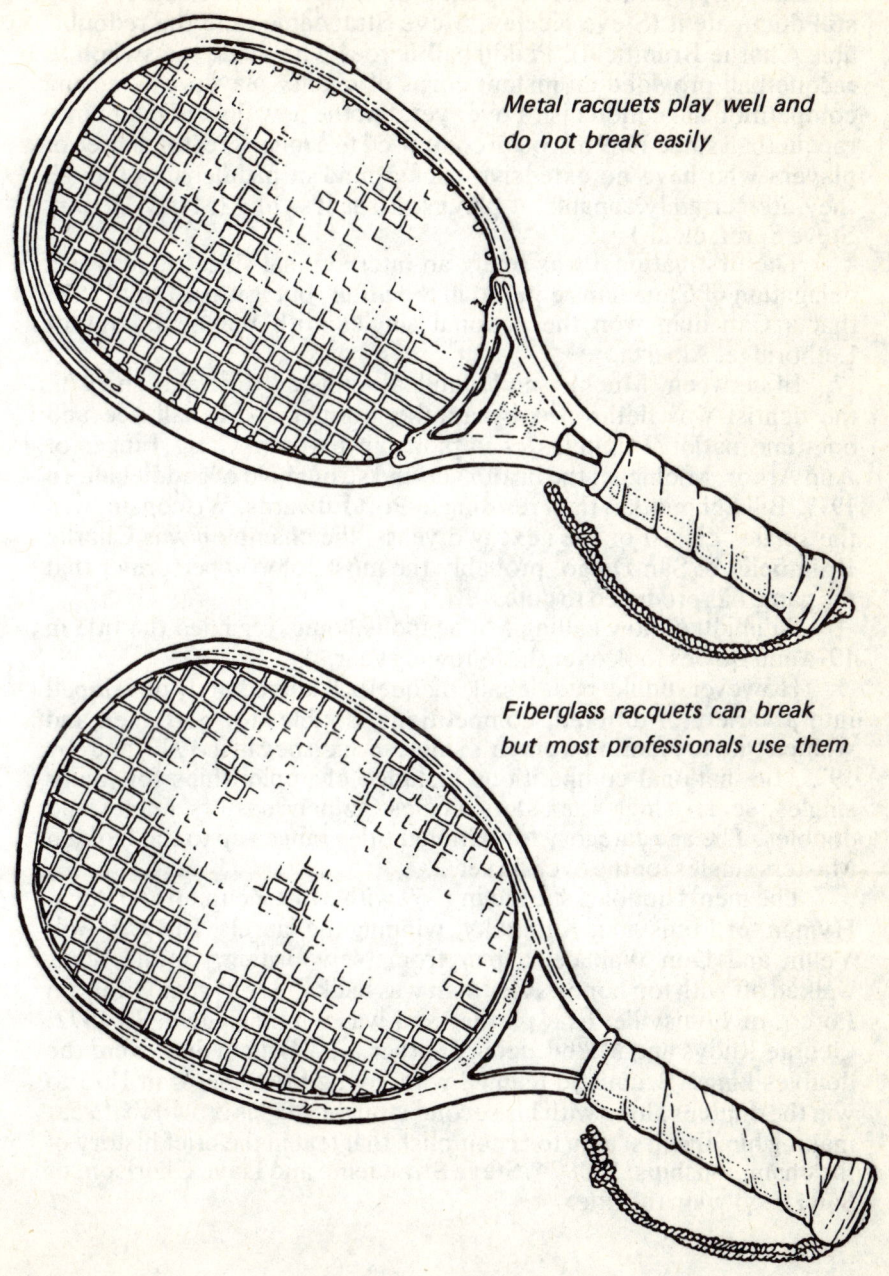

Metal racquets play well and do not break easily

Fiberglass racquets can break but most professionals use them

Muehleisen's pupils and followers made up the early vanguard of outstanding players in the new rage and, to an extensive degree, they still dominate it (Steve Keeley, Steve Strandemo, and the redoubtable Charlie Brumfield). Paddleball heroes who made the switch to racquetball provided an instant corps of quality players and strong competition. The influx isn't over yet, but the new flow of talent into racquetball since 1969 has been composed to a much greater degree of players who have no extensive background in paddleball although they are certainly capable of playing it successfully (Marty Hogan, Steve Serot, et. al.).

The first national was really an international since there was a delegation of Canadians entered in the affair, but it wasn't until 1975 that a Canadian won the national singles with Wayne Bowes of Lethbridge, Alberta.

In between, Muehleisen's pupils dominated the field. In 1970, the dentist was dethroned by another former paddleball ace and one-time national doubles championship partner, Craig Finger of Ann Arbor, Michigan, the birthplace and stronghold of paddleball. In 1971, Bill Schmidtke, then residing in Port Edwards, Wisconsin, was the singles king. For the next two years, the champion was Charlie Brumfield, of San Diego, probably the most colorful performer that the game has produced to date.

Schmidtke, now calling Minneapolis home, regained the title in 1974 and Bowes took over the following year.

However, unlike paddleball, racquetball immediately developed into a variety of different competitions, doubles for both men and women (not to mention women's singles which began in 1970) and, by 1975, the national competitions included championships for junior singles, senior singles, masters singles, golden masters singles and doubles. The age category for national titles ranges up to the Golden Masters singles for the over-55 set.

The men's doubles started in 1969 with Mike Zeitman and Allan Hyman, of Louisville, Kentucky, winning the laurels. In 1970, Bob Yellin and Don Wallace, a pair from New Britain, Connecticut, walked off with top honors. Zeitman was back the next year with Ken Porco, of Louisville, as a partner and was winning again. In 1972, George Rudys and Mike Luciw, another New Britain duo, were the doubles kings. Brumfield teamed with young Steve Serot in 1973 to win the doubles along with his second straight singles crown that year making him the first man to accomplish that feat in the brief history of the championships. In 1974, Steve Strandemo and Dave Charlson, of San Diego, won the title.

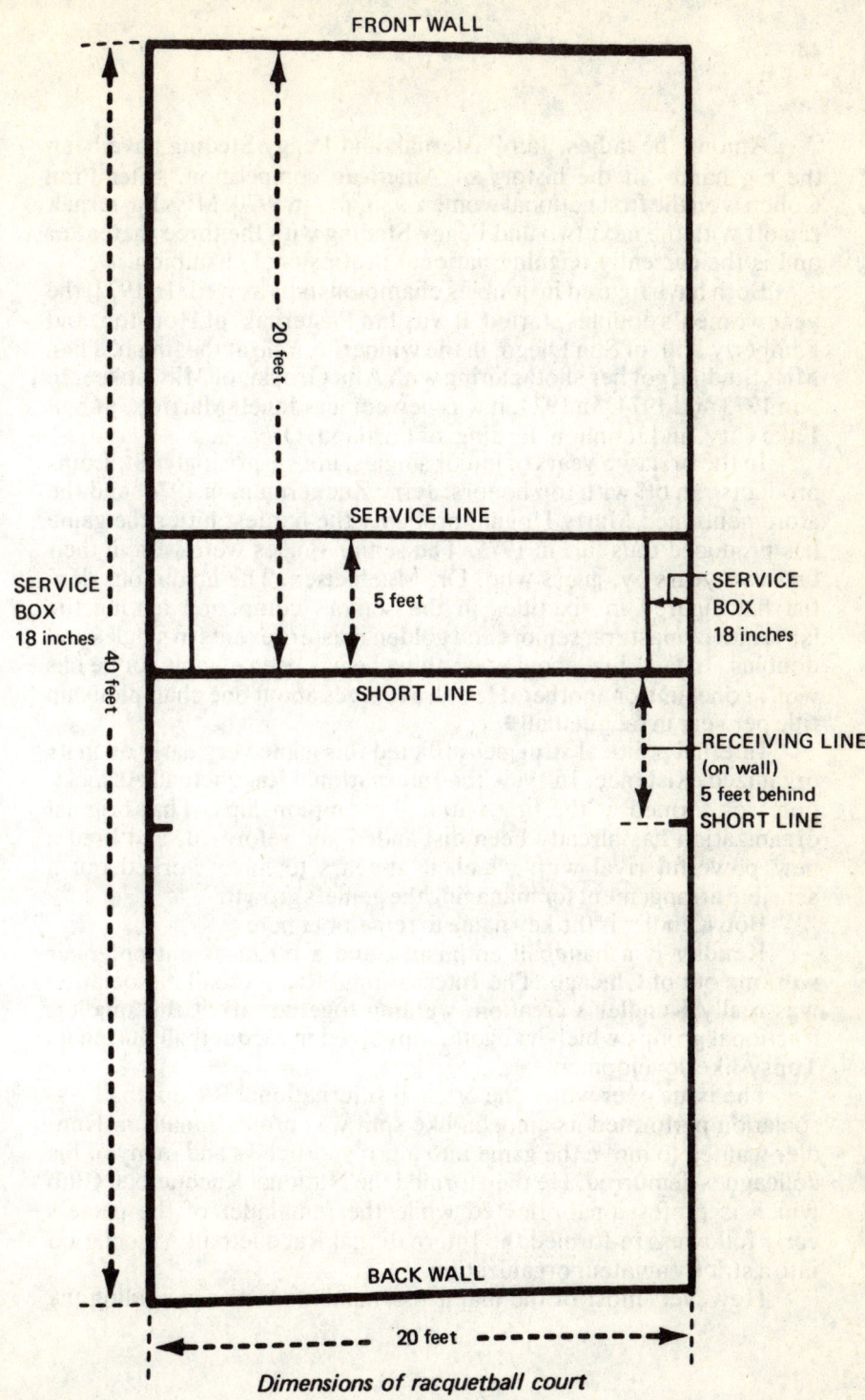

Dimensions of racquetball court

Among the ladies, Jan Pasternak and Peggy Steding have been the big names in the history of American competition. After Fran Cohen won the first national women's singles in 1970, Miss Pasternak ran off with the next two and Peggy Steding with the three thereafter and is the currently-reigning national professional champion.

Both have figured in doubles championships as well. In 1972, the year women's doubles started, it was Jan Pasternak, of Houston, and Kimberly Hill, of San Diego, in the winner's circle at the finish. Then Miss Steding got her shot, pairing with Ann Groski, of Milwaukee, to win 1973 and 1974. In 1974, it was newcomers Janell Marriott, of Salt Lake City, and Jennifer Harding, of Portland, Oregon.

In the first two years of junior singles, not surprisingly, St. Louis products ran off with top honors: Jerry Zuckerman, in 1974, and the aforementioned Marty Hogan, probably the hardest hitter the game has produced thus far, in 1975. The senior singles were won in their first two years by, guess who, Dr. Muehleisen. The ubiquitous dentist has figured in six titles in the seniors competition among the labyrinth of masters, seniors and golden masters events in singles and doubles. In fact, just about everything he has been eligible for he has won at one time or another. He still averages about one championship title per year in racquetball.

Internal political struggles afflicted this game very early on in its organized existence. In 1969, the International Racquetball Association was formed at the first national championships. That original organization has already been disbanded and reformed, and bred a new powerful rival with which it appears to have worked out a sensible arrangement for managing the game's growth.

Bob Kendler is the key name to remember here.

Kendler is a handball enthusiast and a business entrepreneur working out of Chicago. The International Racquetball Association was really Kendler's creation, welding together all of the smaller, fractional groups which had gotten involved in racquetball during its Topsy-like development.

The issue over which the original International Racquetball Association performed its amoeba-like split was professionalism. Kendler wanted to move the game into a pro sport class and many of his colleagues demurred. He then formed the National Racquetball Club which is professional-oriented while the remainder of the game's early followers re-formed the International Racquetball Association into a strictly amateur organization.

However, most of the major tournaments today (including the

nationals) are pro-amateur affairs in which all players can compete on an "open basis."

In 1973, the N.R.C. started its first pro tour. The next year, the I.R.A. joined in with one of its own even though the N.R.C. only played half of the 12 tournaments it had planned for its first tour the year before.

Now both groups are promoting both amateur and pro events with backing from several major corporations, whose roles we will get into shortly.

The tours have shown that several places, largely in the Western half of the country are the early seedbeds for the pro games—Detroit, Chicago, Minneapolis, Houston, Las Vegas and, of course, San Diego and St. Louis. Both tours can be generally expected to appear once in each of these cities.

In its embryonic stage, of course, the pro racquetball tour doesn't provide the kind of prize money which is designed to make pro football stars drool in anticipation. Most of the tournaments in the early years had total purses of something around $10,000 broken down in such a way that the winner made $1,500, the runner-up $1,250, the third-place man $1,000, the losing semifinalist (fourth place) $750 with the rest scattered on down the line.

San Diego leads the country in the number of courts available for the racquetball enthusiast (125 and growing fast) while Chicago is making a strong move into second place ahead of St. Louis. The Windy City in 1975 and 1976 opened 30 new courts, had another dozen already under construction and plans were in the works for about 20 more.

Television exposure is already being planned for some of the major championship tournaments. It seems that the small confines of the court and the high-speed action in both singles and doubles will make professional racquetball something of a television bonanza. However, it faces something of a drawback in that the East Coast, still the most densely populated portion of North America, is conspicuous in its lack of facilities for racquetball and has not manifested the enthusiasm for the game which is evident to the western areas.

Certain parts of New England have evidenced some interest, largely because the game was born in Connecticut. That state, Vermont and, to a lesser degree, New Hampshire, have spawned some fine players.

The nationwide growth from the point of view of numbers of

players is even more impressive than the performance of the professionals in the 1970's. In 1970, there were about 100,000 active racquetball players in the U.S. by best estimates. In four years, that figure grew to 750,000 and by the end of 1976, the number was well over two million, a multiplication of 20 in a mere six years.

Vic Niederhoffer, one of the East's top handball players, a national squash champion and paddleball star, was quoted as saying about racquetball: "In 10 years, it will be bigger than tennis." Tennis, of course, is the fast-growing national and international sport today. Interestingly, Niederhoffer's career in racquetball was brief. Although he was able to reach the national quarterfinals in men's singles in 1975, he retired because he was 32, an age considered a bit old for tournament racquetball, and because of the lack of facilities in the East.

As a recreation, however, racquetball offers opportunities which are not limited by age. Players well into the 50's have found the game to be excellent for recreation and they can keep up with younger men who find the game for more interesting than four-wall paddleball and less taxing than handball. It has the additional advantage of being fairly easy to learn, as contrasted with, say, squash or court tennis, two brethern sports with very complicated rules and styles.

In the next chapter, we will discuss how to play the game.

In general, it may be fairly said that racquetball is easier to master than most of the other racquet sports. The game does not require highly-developed skills of shot-making or a massive awareness of strategy. All of these have helped it to grow rapidly since the rules were standardized in 1968 and the first nationals were held in 1969.

Another factor contributing to the increased popularity of racquet ball is the interest of two major U.S. corporations in the growth of the game. First, Seamco Industries was talked into manufacturing the official racquetball ball, which has a 2½-inch diameter and is made from pressurized rubber. Second, Leach Industries was induced to manufacture the official racquets. Now both corporations have a big stake in racquetball and support it through sponsorship of the two players on the pro tours (Leach sponsors about half of the top 10 men in the N.R.C.) and through contributions to the prize money at the major tournaments. They also help support the game by advertising their products connected with racquetball.

Other recreationally-oriented organizations have also been attracted to racquetball, largely for the purpose of building and promoting the facilities in which the game is played. One of the reasons for this attraction is that the average racquetball court is less expensive,

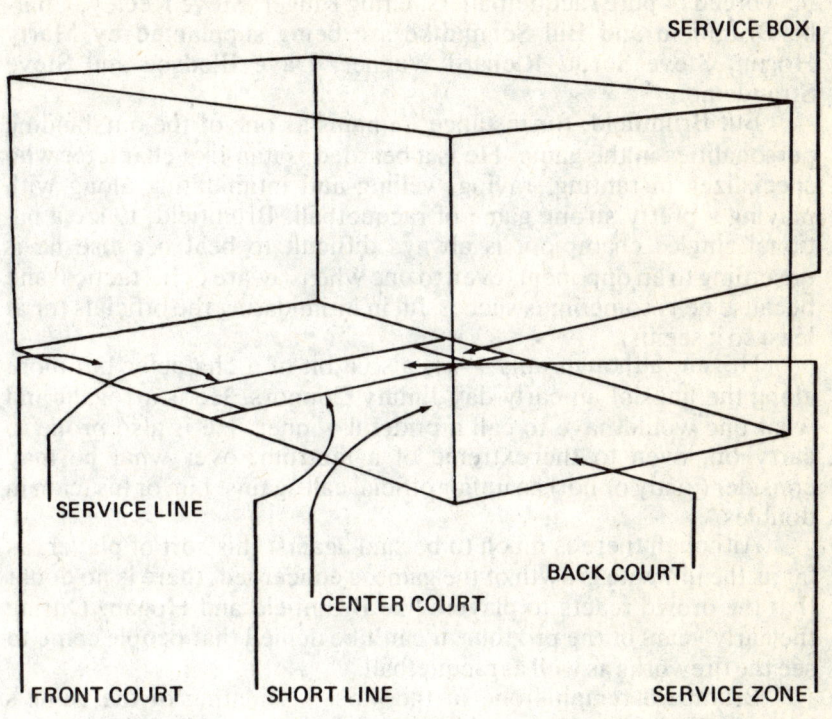

The racquetball court

by half or more, to construct than an indoor tennis court. The average construction price for a racquetball court is now in the area of $75,000, a sum of money that most clubs can afford.

As far as the current state of the game is concerned, many of the outstanding players are beginning to fade and to be replaced by the new breed of pure racquetballers. Craig Finger, Steve Keeley, Charlie Brumfield and Bill Schmidtke are being supplanted by Marty Hogan, Steve Serot, Richard Wagner, Dave Bledsoe and Steve Strandemo.

But Brumfield, for instance, remains as one of the outstanding personalities in the game. He is a bearded, satan-like character who specializes in ranting, raving, yelling and intimidating along with playing a pretty strong game of racquetball. Brumfield, twice a national singles champion, is always difficult to beat because he is unsettling to an opponent (even to one who is aware of his tactics) and because he is sometimes successful in intimidating the officials (or at least so it seems).

Hogan, although only 19, is also a bit of a character but more along the lines of an early-day Jimmy Connors. He is arrogant and what one would have to call a prideful winner. He is also prone to carry on, even to the extreme of a tantrum, over what he may consider (justly or not) an unfair official call against him or his team in doubles.

Although there is much to be said against this sort of player, as far as the ultimate growth of the game is concerned, there is no doubt that the crowd reacts to players like Brumfield and Hogan. During the early years of the pro tour, it can't be denied that people came to see the fireworks as well as racquetball.

Brumfield remains one of the most fascinating of the game's individualist personalities. Although he began to slow down after hitting 28 in 1976, Brumfield was still the only man to capture two successive men's singles national titles in 1972 and 1973. Brumfield won the 1973 championship in the I.R.A. nationals at St. Louis in a match which was considered a classic of its type.

Facing the talented Steve Keeley, also one of the top stars in the game and long a dominant man in paddleball, Brumfield captured the opening game, 21-8. Keeley then responded with an impressive 21-13 rally in the second game to deadlock the match and force it to the decisive third game. Brumfield, pulling out all stops, relentlessly badgered the officials, harassed and obstructed Keeley and finally wrapped up the crown with a 21-12 triumph.

Peggy Steding won the first of her three straight women's crowns that same year in St. Louis by defeating defending champion Jan Pasternak in the finals, 21-19, 21-14. Miss Steding faced one of her stiffest challenges in 1975 when she won the third straight by turning back fellow Texan young Shannon Wright of Dallas, 21-11, 17-21, 21-9, defeating a girl roughly half her age.

By 1975, the expansion in racquetball had created enough matches so that Brumfield was able to continue winning titles even though he had been dethroned in the I.R.A. nationals since 1973.

The 6' 1", 180-pound Brumfield captured the I.R.A. professional championship at St. Louis that year by defeating Steve Serot of San Diego, but not until he survived a first-game blitz by the younger Serot which unnerved the veteran Brumfield. Serot belted Brumfield, 21-13, in the opening game. But, employing his unusual tactics with great aplomb, Brumfield effectively rebounded to unwind Serot in the second game, 21-4. Sensing victory in the offing, Brumfield went for the kill and left Serot in a confused rout, 21-2, in the third game.

A 1970 graduate of the University of San Diego (where he also earned a law degree in 1972 although he has never been a practising lawyer), Brumfield also won the I.R.A. national open doubles in tandem with Craig McCoy of Riverside, California, by defeating two San Diegans, Dave Charlson and Steve Strandemo, 21-20, 21-11.

A month after his 1975 professional championship at St. Louis, Brumfield was in Costa Mesa, Calif., for the national three-wall championship, another new event. Up against a tough field of veteran competitors, the tireless Brumfield again emerged as the champion in the event by clobbering Barry Wallace, a Costa Mesa native, in straight games, 21-15, 21-18. So, even on the downturn of his career, Brumfield continues to be the dominant force in the game and he still can win the championship in any tournament he enters. At one point from 1970 to 1973, Brumfield had won every major invitational tournament in which he was entered.

By 1975, the I.R.A. had expanded into an intercollegiate program which saw national college championships staged at Memphis, Tennessee, home of one of the best collegiate teams, Memphis State. With Frank Woodward, Jim Cullen and Steve Smith, the Tigers swept to the championship. In the men's division A, Smith was the individual champion, with John Lynch of the University of Illinois, the runner-up. In the men's division B, Cullen and Woodward finished first and second.

With 19 points, Memphis State won the team title, Illinois finish-

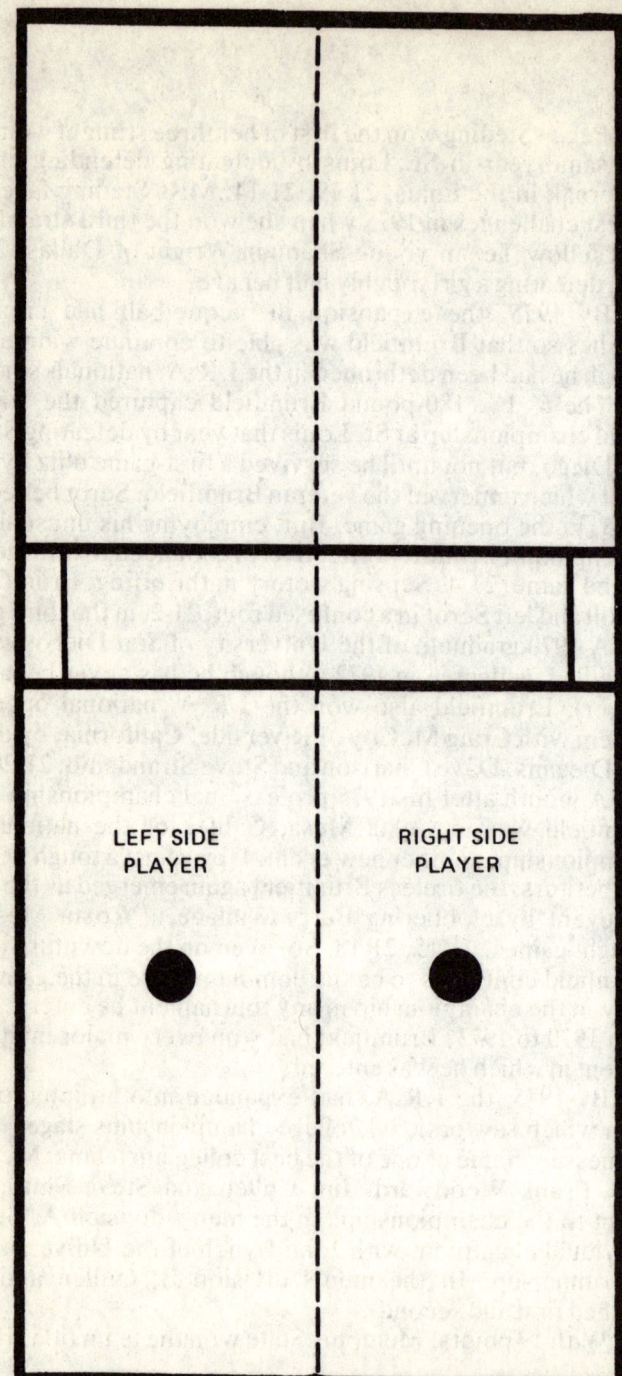

The doubles side-by-side formation

FRONT COURT PLAYER

BACK COURT PLAYER

The doubles front-and-back formation

ing second with 12 and Berea College of Kentucky, third with 6. Memphis State also won the women's title with 8 points, finishing 3 ahead of second-place University of Florida. The University of Tennessee at Chattanooga finished third with 4 points.

In the women's individual competition, Martha Byrd of Florida won the division A crown with Janice Segal of the University of Texas second, while Ellen Jayne of Tennessee finished first in division B, with Memphis State's Diane Palayola the runner-up.

The victory by Wayne Bowes in the I.R.A. open nationals was indicative of the growth of interest in the sport north of the border. Canada's National Klondike Invitational has become one of the major events on the racquetball annual tournament calendar. One of the interesting things about Bowes' triumph was that he beat Trey Sayes of Salt Lake City in the final (16-21, 21-8 21-3). However, the most interesting thing of all was that Charlie Brumfield wasn't a finalist.

Almost from the outset of organized competition, Brumfield has been the key man in the national championships. If you can beat him, you can win the title. Even in 1969, when founding father Bud Muehleisen was the winner, the man he beat in the championship final was Brumfield. The same was true in 1970 when Craig Finger won all the marbles. He, too, had to beat Brumfield in the final.

There might even be something contagious about Brumfield's racquetball play. In 1973, Jan Campbell, Brumfield's girlfriend was ranked third in the nation and rated a shot at the women's open title. She was knocked out of the tournament by Peggy Steding, who, of course, won the ladies' championship.

Of racquetball, Brumfield says, "Of all the court games, racquetball is the fastest and the one I liked the most. The ball travels about 150 miles an hour and on a court where the wall is 20 feet high, the width is 20 feet and the length is 40 feet, you've got to be on your toes all the times.

"But," said Brumfield, perhaps taking note of his own sometimes outrageous tactics, "court games are more mental than physical. To be successful in any of these games, you have to be a defensive, rather than an offensive, player. Offense comes and goes. But defense is something you have to master."

This may be considered sound advice for almost all of the racquet sports. The defensive aspects of court and racquet competition, like most games, are of paramount importance to success.

Although he was also a national paddleball singles king, Brumfield says he prefers racquetball because "you can learn more quickly

FRONT COURT

CENTER COURT

BACK COURT

The three areas of a racquetball court

with the lighter, easier to manage, racquet." When asked if he thought he has a chance to successfully defend his national pro title against the up-and-coming squad of powerful young contenders in 1977, Brumfield answered in the affirmative and said, "I will be totally obnoxious."

If the combination of intimidation and skill can produce a victory, put your money on Charlie Brumfield.

However, the majority of participants in racquet sports (including racquetball) do not play to win titles but for fun and relaxation plus exercise. The points that Brumfield makes about the game and style of racquetball as opposed to some other court games are echoed by most of his fellow players who have shifted over from some other games.

Steve Keeley, also a former national paddleball king, was introduced to Brumfield at the 1970 paddleball nationals in Fargo, North Dakota, and now says, "the future for . . . racquetball is that of a potential blaze."

Another enthusiast for the game is Vic Neiderhoffer. "There aren't many other ways in which an older individual can get exercise after college. Tennis is 80 percent waiting between points. There's no comparison, in terms of use of the body and enjoyment, between jogging and racquetball: one is exercise; the other, athletics. And squash is too difficult and intricate. People want to make the least effort for the most results."

Since Neiderhoffer's last statement certainly has a ring of truth about it, let's move on to the next chapter and find out how to play racquetball.

chapter 4

How to Play Racquetball

BECAUSE RACQUETBALL IS AKIN to paddleball, there are naturally similarities in the approach to the game. But the speed of the ball and the differences in both equipment and rules make those similarities less than might be imagined. Both games are, however, four-wall in their concept, although the one-wall version of handball (which will be discussed in following chapters) is now somewhat more popular than the original four-wall paddleball.

It is obvious and should always be kept in mind, that when one speaks of four-wall racquetball what is actually meant is that the game is played on six sides since the floor and ceiling are, like squash, used in play as well. This can, on occasion, be important.

The ultimate objective of racquetball is to develop, through strategy and position, an effective "kill shot" which will score points for you. Most points in racquetball are scored in this manner.

To begin our discussion of racquetball, let us first examine the equipment involved. Of paramount importance, naturally, is the racquet. Racquetball racquets, like most other phases of this relatively new game, have changed in the past few years. The racquets of a decade ago, with the game still in its infancy, were equipped with a very small striking area surrounded by a thick wood rim mounted at the end of a short handle which tended to inhibit wrist action. Today's racquets are either wood, fiberglass or metal alloy. Most players now prefer the fiberglass and metal alloy racquets over the old wooden version. However, the wood racquets are generally lower priced, and a novice might wish to invest in one while making certain that he likes the game and can play it.

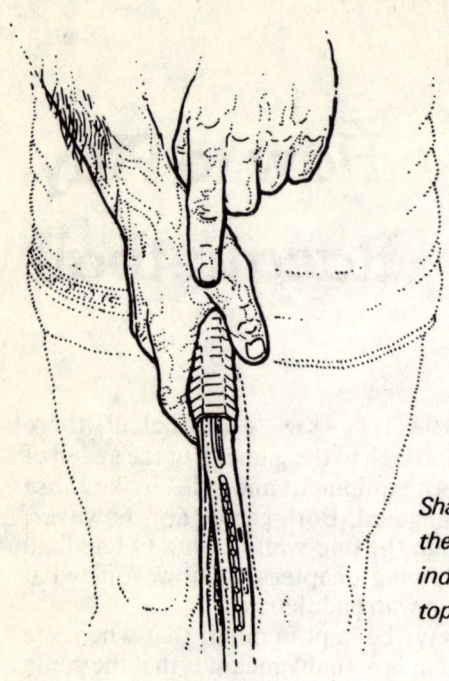

Shaking hands with the racquet: the V formed by the thumb and index finger straddles the handle's topmost surface

Place the thumb between the first two fingers

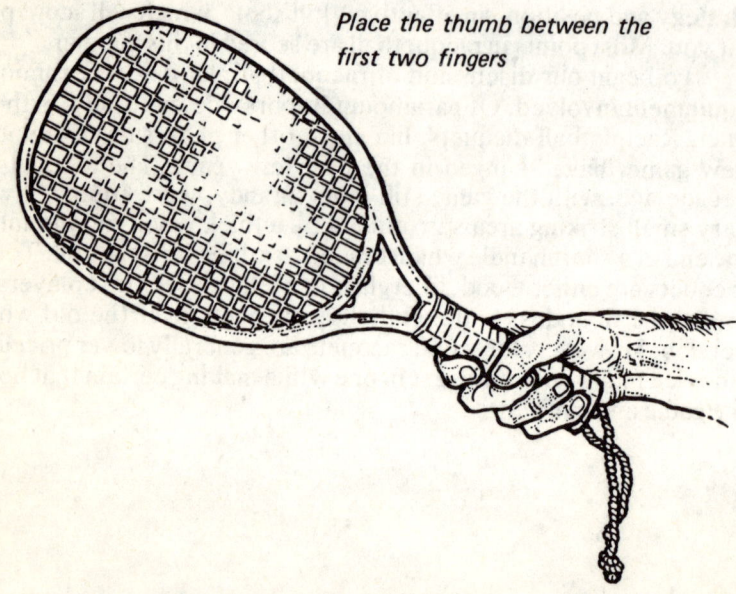

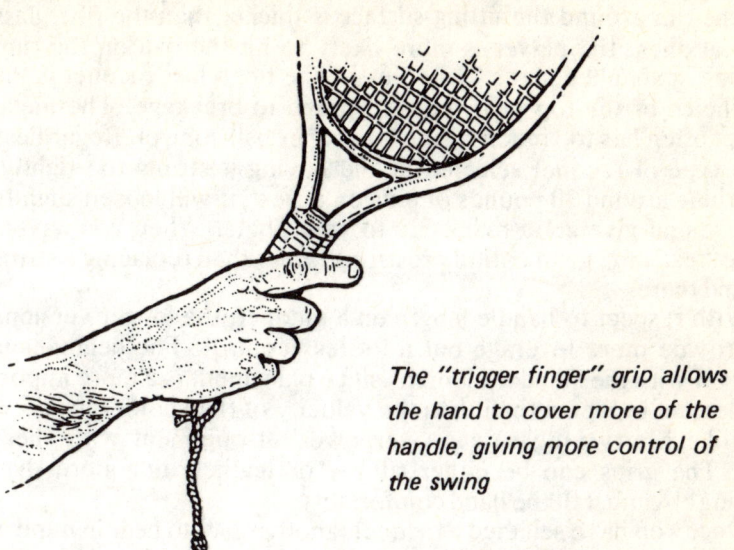

The "trigger finger" grip allows the hand to cover more of the handle, giving more control of the swing

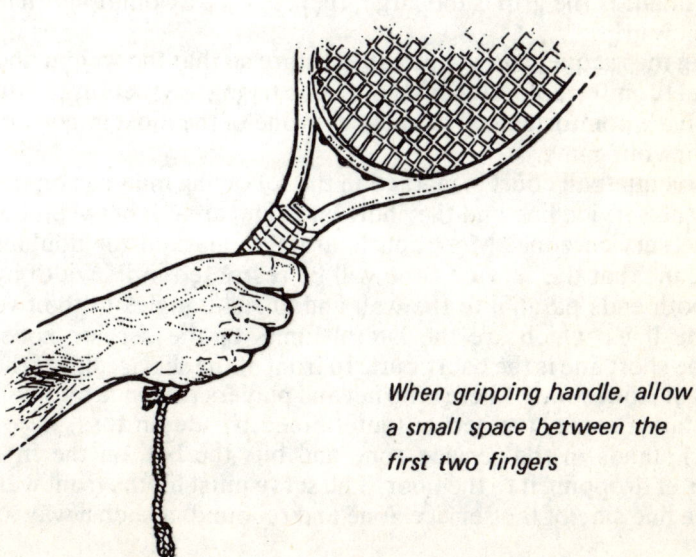

When gripping handle, allow a small space between the first two fingers

Each racquet has its problems. The wood has the most serious since the rim around the hitting surface is thicker than the fiberglass or metal ones, the player is more likely to hit the ball on the rim, resulting in shanked shots "woodies". The fiberglass racquet is the first choice of the top pros, but are prone to breakage. The metal racquet often has too much spring for proper ball control. Regardless of the type of racquet selected, avoid having it strung too tightly. Something around 30 pounds of tension is best, it will loosen slightly with use and give good resiliency to your shots. When you have a racquet restrung, get it entirely restrung rather than replacing a string here and there.

With respect to handle length on a racquet, the longer versions will provide more leverage but a lot less control. The beginner is better off with the standard lengths since placement is a more important element in racquetball than the velocity of the shot. Only a few pros (like Marty Hogan) can overpower an opponent with sheer force. The grips can be either rubber or leather, but more than anything else must fit the hand comfortably.

Once you have selected a racquet, another fact to bear in mind is that the swinging stroke for racquetball is much closer to a golf swing than it is to the standard tennis swing, even on overhead shots. As a consequence, you may want to start with a smaller golf club-sized grip on the racquet, which can always be built up with athletic tape if it feels too small. If the grip is too large, there is no way out other than buying a new grip.

Swing the racquet a few times at the store so that the weight and balance feel comfortable. If they don't, keep trying racquets until you find one that's comfortable. The racquet is one of the most important elements in your game.

The racquetball court is marked in the following manner: on the floor are the service line and the short line. The area in between the two is the service zone. Most courts are also marked for doubles which means that the service zone will be restricted in its width by lines at both ends parallel to the wall and at right angles to the two court-wide lines which are the lateral limits of the service zone. Behind the short line is the backcourt. In front of the service line is the forecourt or front court. There is no net and players play side by side.

To start a game, the server (determined by a coin toss, lot or whatever) stands in the service zone and hits the ball on the first bounce after dropping it to the floor. The serve must hit the front wall on service line side of the service zone and rebound in such a way as

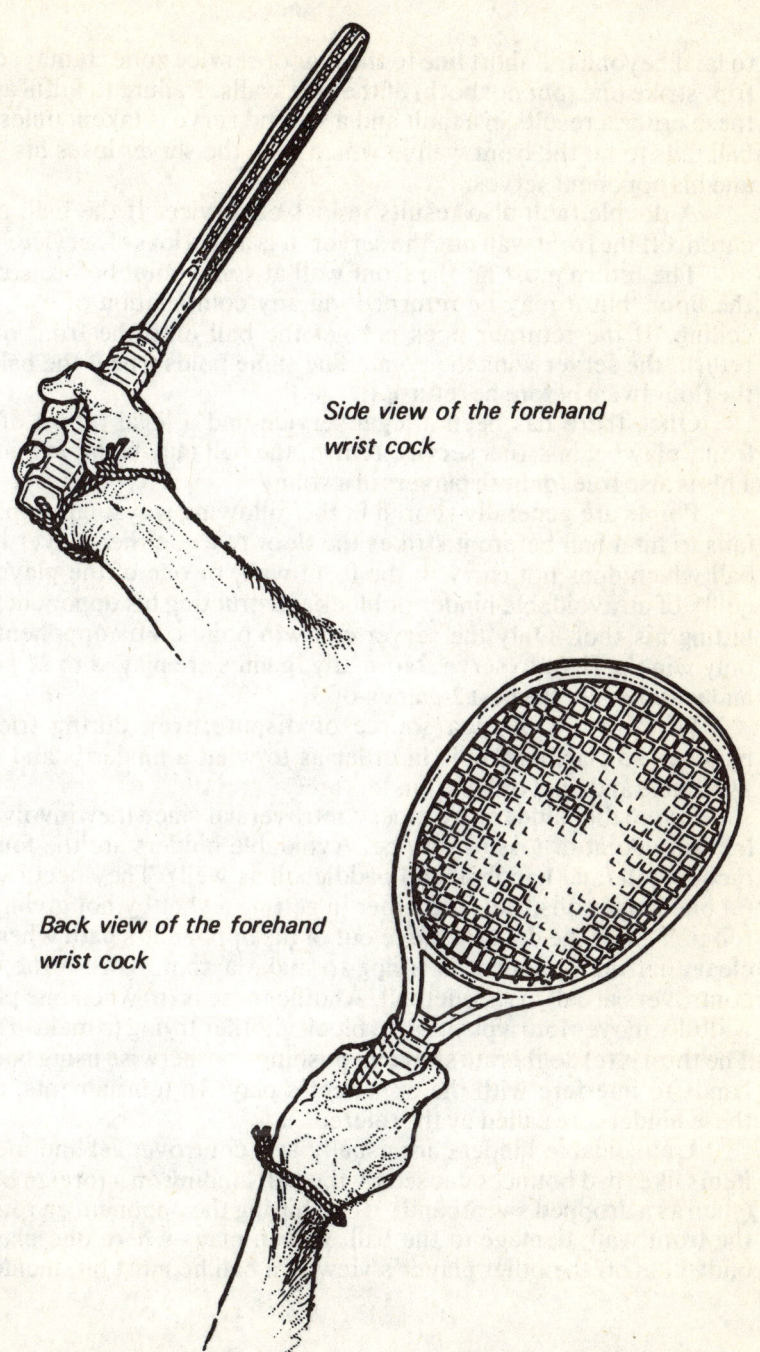

Side view of the forehand wrist cock

Back view of the forehand wrist cock

to land beyond the short line to the rear of service zone. It may, on its trip, strike one (but not both) of the side walls. Failure to fulfill any of these criteria results in a fault and a second serve is taken, unless the ball fails to hit the front wall in which case the server loses his serve and his opponent serves.

A double fault also results in loss of service. If the ball, on its carom off the front wall hits the server, it is also a loss of service.

The return must hit the front wall at some point before striking the floor, but it may be returned via any combination of walls and ceiling. If the returner does not get the ball onto the front on his return, the server wins the point. The same holds true if the ball hits the floor twice before he returns it.

Once there has been a legal service and a legal return off the front, play begins. In a service return, the ball may be hit in mid-air. This is also true for both players in a volley.

Points are generally scored in the following ways: either player fails to hit a ball before it strikes the floor twice, either player hits a ball which does not carry to the front wall, or one of the players is guilty of an avoidable hinder or block, obstructing his opponent from hitting his shot. Only the server can win points. His opponent can only win the right to serve. Normally, games are played to 21 points and matches are the best 2-games-of-3.

Hinders are often a source of dispute even during friendly matches so clarification is in order as to what a hinder is and what avoidable and unavoidable hinders are.

Avoidable hinders are most controversial since they involve the loss of a point or loss of service. Avoidable hinders are the fouls of racquetball (and handball and paddleball as well). They occur when (a) one player obstructs the other in getting a shot by not giving him room. That is, he doesn't move out of his opponent's path when it is clear that the opponent is trying to make a shot. This is the most controversial call in racquetball. Another case is (b) when one player willfully moves into a position to block another trying to make a shot. The third is (c) deliberate shoving, pushing or otherwise using body or hands to interfere with the opponent's play. In tournaments, all of these hinders are called by the referee.

Unavoidable hinders are usually less controversial and include items like: bad bounces caused by the ball landing on a foreign object (such as a dropped sweatband) a ball hitting the opponent en route to the front wall, damage to the ball, screen plays where one player's body cuts off the other player's view of a ball he must hit, incidental

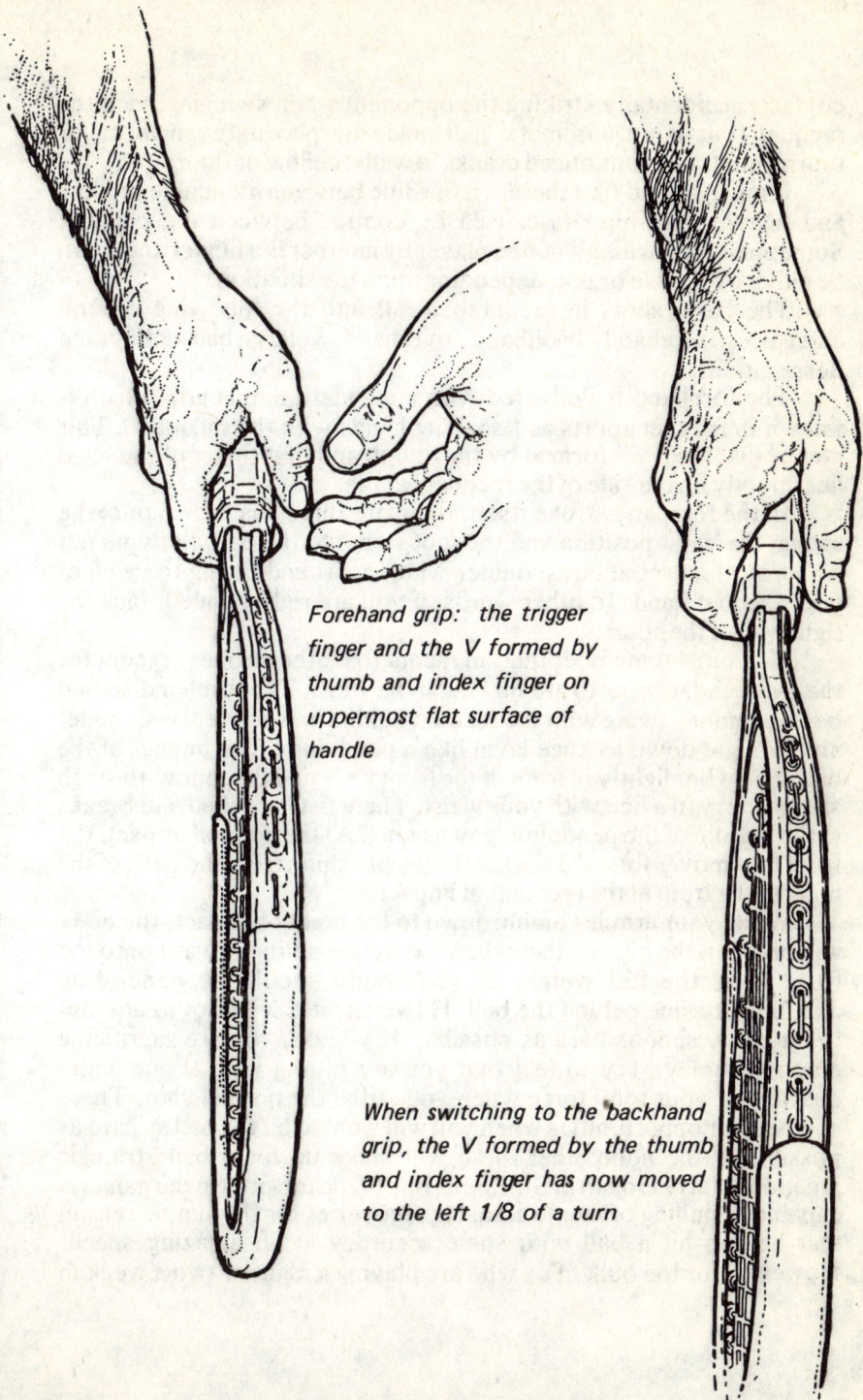

Forehand grip: the trigger finger and the V formed by thumb and index finger on uppermost flat surface of handle

When switching to the backhand grip, the V formed by the thumb and index finger has now moved to the left 1/8 of a turn

contact, accidentally striking the opponent when swinging back the racquet (this is an automatic call made by players even in major tournaments) and unnoticed cracks in walls, ceiling or floor.

It must be said that there is a fine line between avoidable hinders and unavoidable hinders caused by contact between the players. Sometimes "crowding" of one player by another is a hinder and it can be either avoidable or not, depending upon the situation.

The basic shots in racquetball fall into the following general categories: forehand, backhand, overhead, volley, half-volley and desperation.

The forehand is delivered with a standard tennis grip which is known in racquet sports as "shaking hands with the racquet". This means that the "V" formed by the thumb and first finger of the hand lies directly on the side of the racquet handle.

In the forehand stroke itself, there are three basic elements, the swing, the wrist position and the foot step into the ball. Set yourself with your feet set about shoulder-width apart and facing the wall of your racquet hand. In other words, if you are right-handed, face the right wall of the court.

You must remember that, in racquetball, the strokes (except for the overhead, of couse) are hit below the waist. The forehand should be one smooth swing with the racquet behind and above the shoulder and brought down to knee level like a pendulum. The impact of the ball should be slightly in front of the front knee and the follow-through should carry in a line with your waist. The wrist is cocked and breaks at the bottom of the pendulum downswing. At the point of impact, the front foot moves forward so that the weight shifts from the back of the body to the front at the moment of impact.

While your arm is coming down to the point of impact, the body will pivot on the hips so that when the weight shifts forward onto the front foot, the full weight of your body should be generating maximum torque behind the ball. However, it is wise not to attempt to hit every shot as hard as possible. If you do, you are sacrificing much accuracy. Try to feel that you are hitting with about three-quarters of your total force when you strike the normal shot. There will be clear opportunities when you will want to hit the ball as hard as possible in the hopes that force will make up for a bad strategic position. Marty Hogan of St. Louis, one of the top pros in the game, is capable of pulling off some amazing recoveries for the simple reason that he can hit a ball with some accuracy at an amazing speed. However, for the bulk of us who are playing a night or two a week in

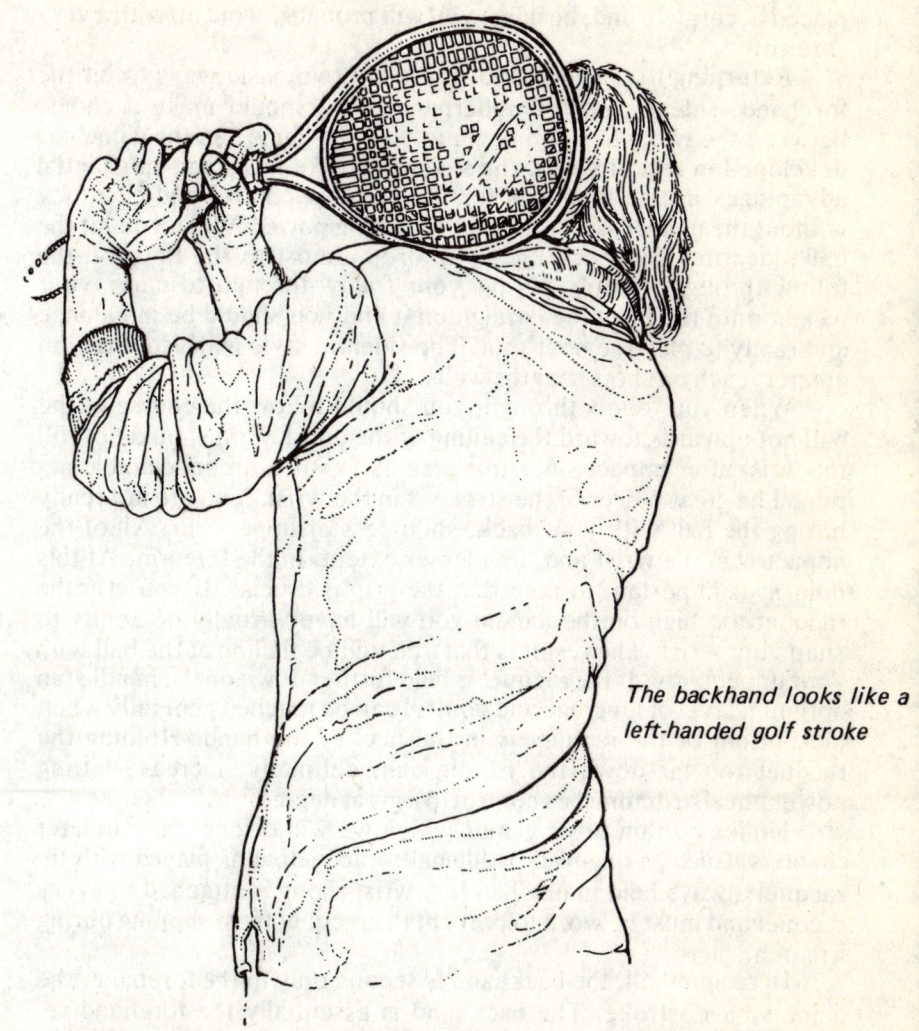

The backhand looks like a left-handed golf stroke

the name of good fellowship, exercise and recreation, this is not a possibility. Therefore, curb your impulse to slam every shot with all your might. It doesn't win as many points as a well-stroked ball placed accurately and, besides, you will probably wind up with a very sore arm.

Returning to the forehand, there are two basic ways to hit the forehand, sidearm and/or underhand. You should make a choice between the two when you begin to play the game. As the game has developed in recent years, the sidearm stroke has some substantial advantages in that it allows for the greatest control and accuracy without the unnecessary sacrifice of hitting power. When you hit the ball sidearm, your back knee will drop almost to the floor on the follow-through. Simply permit your follow-through to carry your weight onto the front leg, straighten it and you should be in balance and ready to play the next shot. The sidearm style will also give you greater reach on shots near the walls.

When you follow through, you should follow the course of the ball not upwards toward the ceiling of the court. You should not roll the wrist after impact since this creates topspin, an undesirable action. The great power of the stroke is in the wrist. You are not really hitting the ball with your back, shoulders or upper arm. All of the impact is in the wrist and, to a lesser extent, in the forearm. At this point it is important to note that the grip is crucial. If you grip the racquet too high on the handle you will have virtually no ability to snap your wrist. The result is that you will be flailing at the ball with your upper body. If the racquet is held further down on the handle, an optimum level of leverage and control can be reached generally when the bottom of the racquet is in the heel of the hand. Holding the racquet too far down the handle can, definitely, increase hitting power but also diminishes control to a great degree.

Unlike certain other games which we will discuss here in later chapters, (such as one-wall paddleball), racquetball is played with the racquet always held in one hand. A wrist thong is attached to every racquet and must be worn to prevent the racquet from slipping during a match.

In racquetball, the backhand is second only to the forehand, the game's basic stroke. The backhand is essentially the forehand reversed with a couple of significant differences. Major among these is the grip. All of the game's outstanding players make the same basic adjustment—they rotate their grip about 12½ percent downward on the backhand. This keeps the racquet face from opening up toward

Full-overhead swing at point where ball is hit

the front wall which will give the ball an unwanted loft and cause it to float.

By virtue of the slight downturn on the racquet handle, the backhand stroke will retain most of the zip of the forehand and should, with a little practice, enable the player to keep complete accuracy on his backhand. Bear in mind that you can use your free hand to turn the racquet when the adjustment in the grip is being made between the forehand and the backhand or vice-versa. Be sure that the top of the racquet face is pointing toward the front wall on all shots and you can put the ball where you want it to go.

The other major difference in the backhand shot is that the point of impact is slightly further away from the body, being generally just below the front knee and, for most players, just beyond the tip of the shoe on your forward foot. Otherwise, the action of the body is basically the same as the forehand except in reverse. The follow-through will pivot the hip around, the back knee will drop as the weight shifts to the front foot on the impact with the ball and the wrist-snap provides the bulk of the power.

Anyone with some exposure to golf will observe in these basic strokes a close similarity between the body action in the golf shot and the racquetball stroke. From this standpoint, the two games are somewhat complimentary.

One of the most important points to remember as you start learning to play racquetball is that you should always try to hit the ball from a convenient position. Place yourself so that you can easily return the next ball. The game should be fun and exercise, with a healthy dash of competition thrown in for good measure, not a chore to be performed. But the basic guidelines of how to hit the ball apply to everyone with minor adjustments for the individual.

Of course there are a variety of other shots in racquetball with which you should be familiar, but before proceeding with them we will pause to discuss some general thoughts about strategy. One of the basic ideas of the game is to produce shots in some combination which will enable you to position yourself for a kill (or non-returnable) shot while, simultaneously, keeping your opponent out of position so that he becomes vulnerable to the shot. This is most frequently done through the effective use of what are known as complementary shots. Put simply, this means that if you serve and your opponent successfully returns the service, you (still possessing the advantage as the server) will probably be able to direct the course of the ball with your first volley shot. If your serve was decent, your opponent will be slightly off balance after returning the ball since you know where the serve is going and he doesn't. This same general thinking applies to tennis and almost all other racquet and court games.

Complementary shots are the combination of shots which keep your opponent in that off-balance position. In other words, if you hit your first volley high off the left side of the front wall, you would want to direct your next shot low on the right side to keep your opponent constantly in motion. Vary the pattern of your shots and don't let the opponent get a feeling of rythm in your game. The mental exercise of the game consists of staying one play ahead of your opponent. Once you have set up your opponent for the kill shot, try to hit the ball into the lower corner of the front wall on your forehand side. The kill shot is hit like the forehand, but to be effective it must be hit at ankle height with a good velocity.

But the kill shot is the end of the expedition. The first trick is to get that far. Starting with the serve, of which there are four general varieties, and progressing into the volleys we have several other shots to examine. The four basic serves are the lob, the half lob, the drive and the Z. The importance of the service can not be overly stressed, especially since the high-speed game of racquetball is not prone to lengthy rallies like tennis. In a normal situation, a point will last about four shots, starting from the serve. One well-placed shot will usually win a point, except in a tournament game, so if that well-placed shot is also the serve, you have saved yourself an enormous amount of time.

The most effective serve is the drive shot when it is properly executed. Start from the center of the service box and make contact at knee level or lower. Give the serve a full 75-80% power and try to hit the front wall about 3 feet up from the floor just to the left (or right if you are lefthanded) of center. The so-called "Z" serve is the next best choice. It is easier to deliver than a solid drive and almost as effective. The basic idea of the Z-serve is to deliver the ball off the front wall, onto the floor and into a side wall low enough down that the return of service will be either feeble or non-existent. It should be pointed out that a service itself seldom wins a point. In other words, unlike tennis, aces are rarely served in racquetball. But a good serve will produce a weak return of service and, on the first volley, the server should be able to put away his victim. Whenever possible you serve to the opponent's backhand on the general theory that all players are weaker on the backhand than they are on the forehand.

This maneuver is used by the best pros in the game, so it will work for the novice as well.

On the Z-serves, there are basically four choices, although only three of them are really viable alternatives. Two of them are called "reverse Z's" since they are to the backhand of the opponent, either low and hard or high and soft. The low, hard Z is hit about 3 feet high and about a foot from the side wall nearest your opponent's backhand while the high, soft Z is hit about 5-6 feet off the front wall and a foot or so from the side wall on his backhand side. The other two Z's are to the forehand, also low, hard and high, soft. The low, hard to the forehand is a very poor choice of service since it practically invites a strong return to the server's backhand, shifting the balance of play from the server to the returner. The high, soft Z to the forehand is executed as the high, soft Z to the backhand except it is hit on the front wall about a foot from the wall nearest the opponent's forehand. Both of the high, soft serves are best executed with about 50% power.

Knowing a wide variety of serves are not essential to winning racquetball. The key here is to learn how to place the ball when you serve. Charlie Brumfield, probably the most consistent winner the game has produced to date, thrives on the half-lob serve which is called in the trade the "garbage serve". The server simply hits the ball off the front wall with a pushing motion contacted about chest aimed halfway up the wall, a foot or so off-center, to the receiver's backhand side. With a deft touch, this serve simply drops dead to the floor and feebly rolls away making a return impossible or acrobatic. The full lob, on the other hand, is contacted at the same point (about chest high) but is hit more firmly, about three-fourths of the way up the front wall slightly to the receiver's backhand side of center. It should hit the backhand sidewall of the receiver about 6 to 8 feet in from the backwall and about 5 or 6 feet from the floor. It is not a first choice for service either for the beginner or fairly experienced player.

The return of service offers three general options, the best of which is the ceiling ball. This is the ball hit between 1 to 5 feet off the front wall onto the ceiling. It then shoots down onto the front wall, continues down to the floor and will render the server no real options for returning the ball. Since it normally lands so high, his only option will be another ceiling ball, allowing the receiver to get set. If the server presents a ball which can be hit for a drive, low and hard, that is done either off the forehand or the backhand. Another good return is a three-wall ball in which the receiver of the service hits the ball high into the corner, preferably (for him) off his forehand about 2 feet from

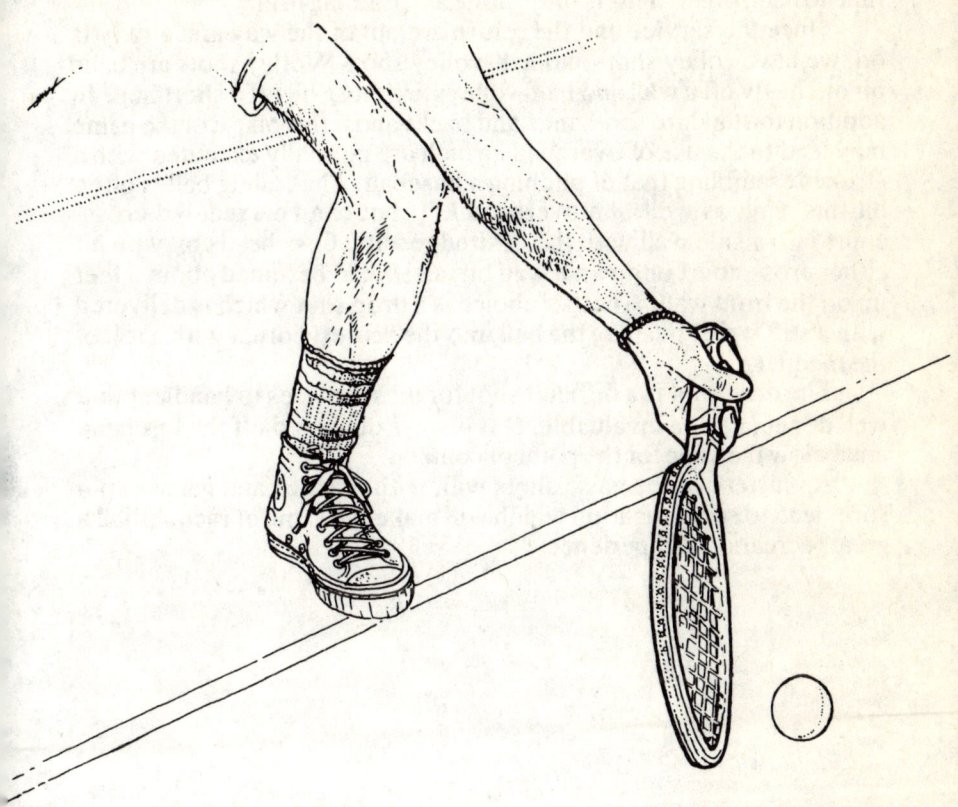

The drop shot

the front wall. When the ball hits the sidewall high in the corner, it ricochets into the front wall, then caroms to the other sidewall around the middle of the court and, then, heads back toward the low opposition corner from whence it was delivered. It is possible for two men to stand side by each and hit the ball around the walls for an indefinite time to each other. This is often done as a training drill.

Once the service and the return are out of the way and a rally is on, we have volley shots and half-volley shots. Volley shots are balls hit on the fly off a wall and half-volleys are those hit off a short hop. In addition to standard forehands and backhands, this phase of the game may lead to the use of overheads which are normally executed with a stroke resembling that of pitching a baseball. The ceiling ball is often hit this way, as well. An overhead kill shot can be executed cross-court into a side wall with the desired results. Overheads may be hit either cross-court or down a wall but all should be aimed about 3 feet up on the front wall. Another choice is a drop shot which is delivered with a stiff wrist, pushing the ball into the nearest corner with a roll of the racquet.

The drop shot is a difficult shot for most novices to handle, but if well done it can be invaluable. It is always delivered off the forehand and below the knee for the point of contact.

A mastery of the basic shots will, with practice and game exposure, lead to sophistication which will make the game of racquetball a great recreational experience.

chapter 5

Paddleball

PADDLEBALL, THAT PECULIAR COMBINATION of tennis and handball, is a game which has become national in scope. However, there is yet to be a rule-making national association in spite of the fact the game was introduced back in 1930.

The game has been beset by a variety of squabbles among its various associations and groups. These problems certainly curtailed its growth in the beginning. With the recent expansion of interest throughout the country in paddleball, it is hard to imagine how popular the game might have been without all of the fractionalization and sectional rivalry.

For the sake of simplicity, the basic difference between the variety of paddleball games (and hence its differing governing bodies) involves the number of walls used in competition. The National Association conducts all of the major four-wall competitions. This organization is the oldest in the field and had the inventor of the game as its first president. However, in recent years, the one-wall version of the game has become equally as popular as the traditional four-wall version of the game has become equally as popular as the traditional four-wall one and its popularity has spawned two different associations which conduct competitions on a national level.

The one-wall type of paddleball can be played by almost everybody in that most city parks and most college campuses have a wall suitable for competition while the four-wall style of the game requires a regulations four-wall handball-type court. Also, from the spectator point of view, the one-wall sport is easier to follow.

A University of Michigan professor, Earl Riskey, invented paddleball. He was an avid enthusiast of paddle-tennis and began by experimenting with a paddle-tennis racquet and a sponge rubber ball. A regular tennis ball was tried when the sponge rubber one proved to be too heavy, but it, too, was not satisfactory. Since it was the weight of the ball which was causing the problem, Riskey soaked the ball in gasoline, peeled off its felt outer cover and tried the remaining red rubber, air-filled, interior ball. It worked well and the game of paddleball was on its way.

The red ball proved to be much more lively than a tennis ball and because of its color, was also easier to follow during the playing of a match on the handball court. Riskey then adapted standard handball rules to his game—and paddleball was invented. Through the intervening years, several changes have occurred during the game's development, including the creation of a new ball which is dark gray in color and doesn't have the air-filled core of the tennis ball. The removal of the air from the center of the ball gave it a much truer bounce and therefore prolonged the rallies, making paddleball more interesting both to play and watch.

The paddle, too, is now a standard paddleball racquet rather than a paddle-tennis, one. Most racquets are made of plywood and have a series of ventilation holes around the edge, about one inch from the outer rim of the paddle and the paddles are more rectangular than rounded.

Since Riskey developed the game originally in Michigan as a four-wall game, the great bulk of its Midwestern adherents have loyally stayed with the four-wall version. As a result, the hard-core of support for that version of paddleball and the National Association, as well, remains near the birthplace of the game. California, where several former Midwesterners have spread the gospel of the four-wall game, also is solidly behind Riskey's rules.

On the Eastern seaboard, the game is almost universally played as a one-wall sport and since the very early 1960's, two associations—the American and the United States—have tried to organize and govern the one-wall version of the sport. The United States Paddleball Association, based in New York City, was actually the first to try to organize national tournament competition.

It initiated a national singles one-wall tournament in Brooklyn in 1961. The tournament was won by Howard Eisenberg of Brooklyn who dominated tournament play during the early years, winning the men's singles in 1962, 1963 and 1964. Eisenberg's domination was finally broken by two men who have become giants in the one-wall version of the game, Vic Neiderhoffer and Howie Hammer. Neiderhoffer, part of a brother tandem active in handball and other similar games around the New York area, won the national one-wall paddleball men's singles in 1965 and 1966 before being succeeded as champion in 1967 and 1968 by Hammer.

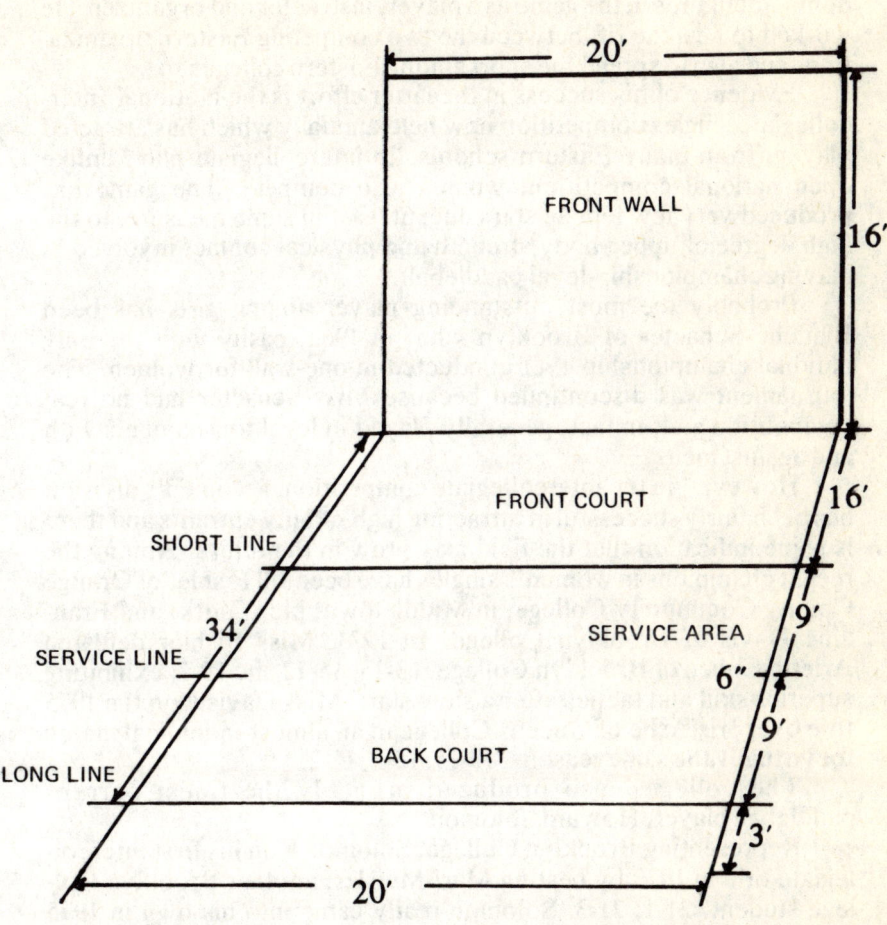

One-wall Paddleball Court Dimensions

Hammer, a physical education instructor at New York's Queensborough Community College, has since become one of the dominant figures in the game as a player, instructor and organizer. He worked to heal the rift between the two competing Eastern organizations and also to spread the sport among Eastern colleges.

Evidence of his success in the latter effort is the National Intercollegiate singles competition now held annually which has attracted players from many Eastern schools. In intercollegiate play, unlike open national competition, women also compete. The game has produced very few female stars due, at least in some measure, to the high degree of upper-body strength and physical contact involved in playing championship-level paddleball.

Probably the most outstanding player among girls has been Blanche Schacter of Brooklyn who, in 1963, easily won the only national championship ever conducted in one-wall for women. The tournament was discontinued because Miss Schacter had no real competition and, in fact, generally played in local tournaments with and against men.

However, in the intercollegiate competition, a women's division has been fairly successful in attracting high-quality entrants and there is some indication that the field may grow in the future. Among the recent champions in women's singles have been Jill Fishler of Orange County Community College, in Middletown, New York, and Francine Davis of Brooklyn College. In 1973, Miss Fishler defeated Arlette Cohen of Brooklyn College, 13-15, 15-12 and 15-7, exhibiting superior skill and tactics after a slow start. Miss Davis won the 1975 title over Iris Ashe of Queens College in an almost-indentical match for virtually the same reasons, 13-15, 15-5, 15-2.

The colleges also produced probably the finest current paddleball player, Howard Solomon.

Representing Brooklyn College, Solomon won his first intercollegiate title in 1973 by besting Mart Meisler, another Brooklyn College student, 21-1, 21-3. Solomon really came into his own in 1975 when he won his third straight intercollegiate championship and also captured the national open one-wall title in the competition conducted by the American Paddleball Association. In the national final, Solomon defeated Tom Lowy of New York, 21-6 and 21-9.

He completed a grand slam of one-wall honors by teaming with Robert Schwarz of Far Rockaway, New York, to beat Lowy and Ken Levine of Brooklyn, 21-14 and 21-3, in the doubles championship. Schwarz, himself, was no newcomer to the national champion-

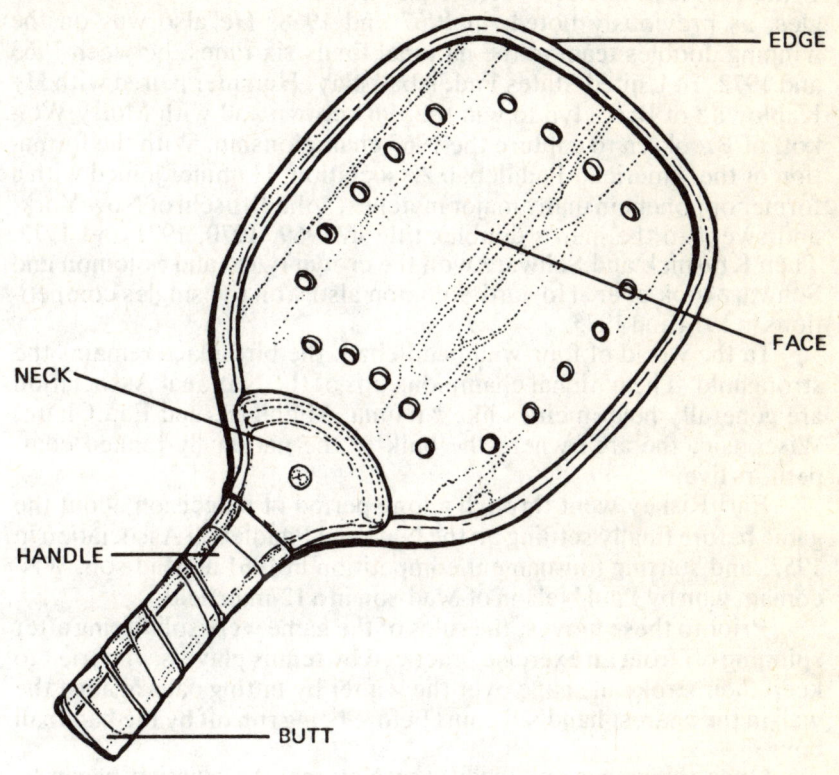

The Paddleball Paddle

ships, having been paired with another Far Rockaway player, Andy Krasnick, in winning the doubles competition in both 1973 and 1974.

Solomon, however, will have to make up appreciable distance before he can close in on the records held by Howie Hammer. Competing originally when the competitions were conducted by the United States Paddleball Association, Hammer won the men's singles, as previously noted, in 1967 and 1968. He also was on the winning doubles team in the national finals six times, between 1963 and 1972. In United States Paddleball play, Hammer paired with Hy Kaplowitz of Brooklyn to win the 1963 crown and with Morty Wolkoff of Brooklyn to capture the 1967 championship. With the formation of the American Paddleball Association, Hammer joined with a former opponent in many major matches, John Bruschi of New York, and swept to the men's doubles title in 1969, 1970, 1971 and 1972. Then Krasnick and Schwarz won the crown twice and Solomon and Schwarz took over. Howard Solomon also won the singles competitions in 1974 and 1975.

In the world of four-wall paddleball, the birthplace remains the stronghold. The national championships of the National Association are generally held in cities like Livonia, Michigan, and Eau Claire, Wisconsin, the area where the bulk of the nationally-ranked competitors live.

Earl Riskey went through a long period of indecision about the game before finally settling on the National Paddleball Association in 1952, and starting tournament competition in 1961 at Madison, Wisconsin, won by Paul Nelson of Madison in a 12-man field.

Prior to these moves, the rules of the game were solidifying after spinning off from an exercise practiced by tennis players who tried to keep their stroke in shape over the winter by hitting balls against the wall in the nearest handball court before being run off by the handball boys.

Once things got organized, the National Association began to hold regular tournaments. In 1962, Nelson won the men's singles and the combination of Maurice Ruben and John Blanchieu won the doubles exercise. Bill Schultz, of Madison, won the singles in 1963 and Nelson captured the title again in 1964 while the doubles in both years went to a brother tandem, Bob and Dick McNamara of Minneapolis.

In 1965, Mobey Benedict took the singles title. The first non-Midwestern winner was Bud Muehleisen, of San Diego, in 1966 and Paul Lawrence of Ann Arbor, Michigan, took the crown back in

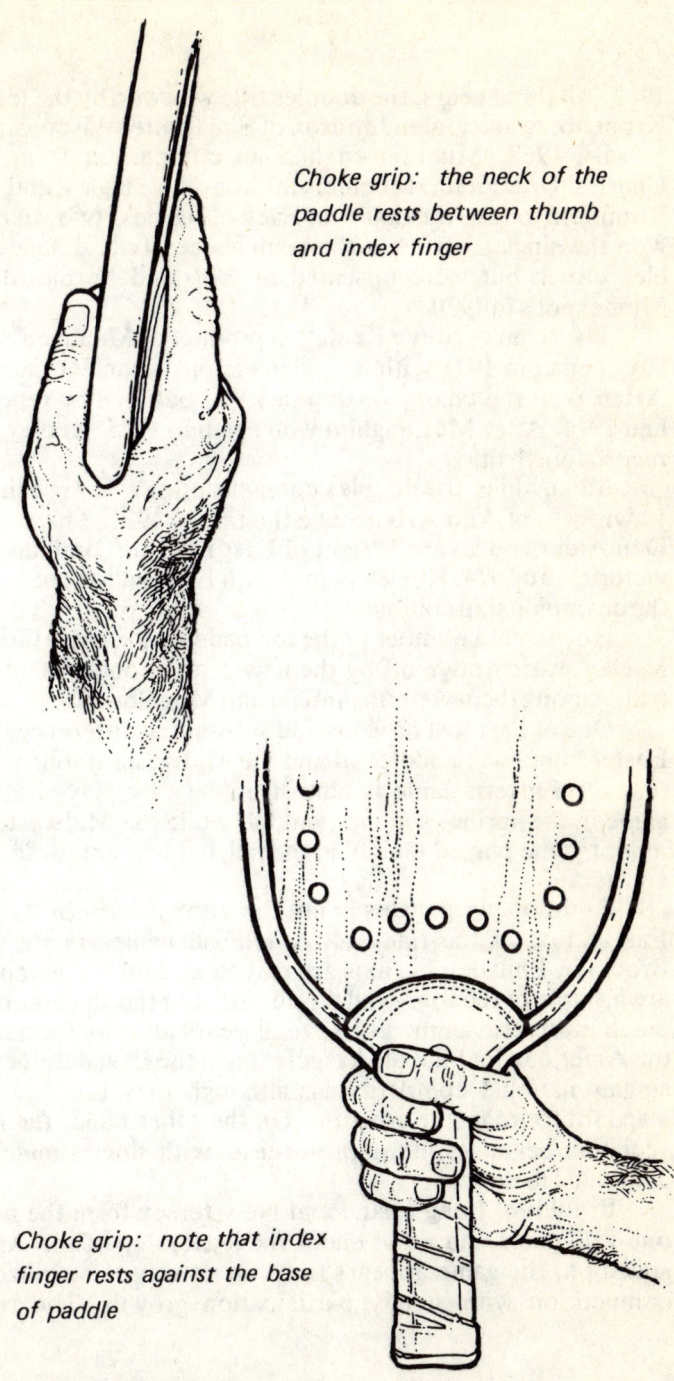

Choke grip: the neck of the paddle rests between thumb and index finger

Choke grip: note that index finger rests against the base of paddle

1967. All three years, the doubles title was won by the team of Harold Kronenberg and Galen Johnson of Eau Claire, Wisconsin.

By 1968, Muehleisen had an companion from San Diego, Charles Brumfield. Muehleisen won the singles and paired with Brumfield to take the doubles. Each of the next two years, Brumfield won the singles. In 1969, the team successfully defended their doubles crown but were unseated by Bob and Bernie McNamara of Minneapolis in 1970.

The reign of Steve Keeley, a product of Michigan State University, began in 1971 with a singles victory. Dan McLaughlin of Ann Arbor won the championship in 1972, but Keeley repeated in 1973 and 1974. After McLaughlin won again in 1975, Keeley captured his record fourth title.

Meanwhile, the doubles competition saw Craig Finger and Paul Lawrence, of Ann Arbor, take the title in 1971. The next two years, Dan Alder and Evans Wright of East Lansing combined for doubles victories. In 1974, Keeley paired with Len Baldori, of San Diego, for the championship combination.

However, a number of the top paddleball competitors, including Keeley, were drawn off by the new professional circuits in racquetball. Among them were Brumfield and Muehleisen.

One of the most obvious and substantial differences between the Eastern one-wall paddleball and the Midwestern four-wall vairety is that the Eastern game is almost universally played as an outdoor game in the spring, summer and fall while the Midwestern one is an indoor game played mainly in the fall and winter months on handball courts.

Additionally, singles is not the normal form of the game in the East. Most of the one-wall paddleball games in the New York-Brooklyn-Philadelphia axis are played as doubles matches. Doubles are a staple of the four-wall world, too, but the singles competition is much more prevalent. For several years after its formation in 1969, the American Paddleball Association in the East didn't even conduct singles national competitions, although they are now part of the standard tournament program. On the other hand, the national Association began its life, more-or-less, with singles matches and has continued to do so.

Brooklyn, Long Island and New Jersey form the hotbed of the one-wall game and now, under the leadership of the American Association, the game appears to be on its way to stabilized rules and competition with steady participation growth. The rules for the

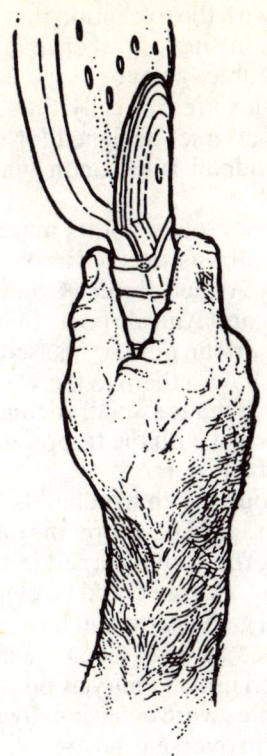

Eastern grip, front view: shake hands with the paddle, much the same as the tennis grip

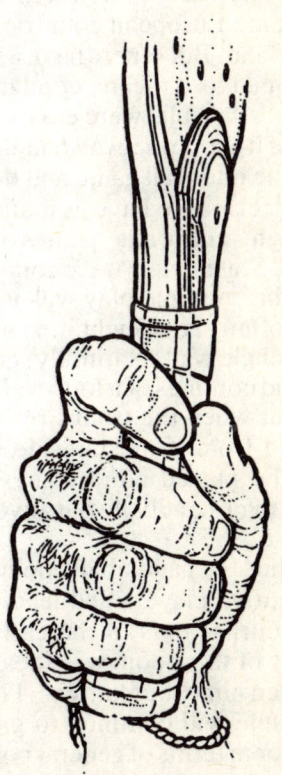

Eastern grip, back view

American Association are generally drawn for doubles, although the same rules apply to singles games with the exception that a server may serve from anywhere on the court in singles rather than from a more restricted designated area in the doubles game.

The National Association rules are basically those of handball with a few exceptions and are, of course, designed for use by either singles or doubles as are the handball rules upon which they are based.

The game of paddleball doubles really got its major shot in the arm during World War II. Paddleball was selected as one of the major recreational activities for the U.S. Armed Forces Conditioning Program at the University of Michigan (Ann Arbor). During the war years, thousands of men in the American military passed through this program and carried the game away with them to the various installations where they were stationed. Because small racquets and balls were used, the game even went aboard with the troops and it could be played anywhere there was a handball court.

Some European countries abound with handball facilities, notably Ireland. But others have a shortage. Therefore, the one-wall game developed as a means of adapting the skills learned in the four-wall paddleball. Walls were easy to find, an area could be cleared away in front of it and a one-wall paddleball game gotten underway.

The one-wall game and doubles got married in the military since the object was to have as many men use a facility as possible. In fact, although "cutthroat" games of triples were occasionally played in the United States, they were common in overseas posts.

This multiple play was used as a field expedient during the war when often six or eight men at a time played a game with a lone ball and a single wall. Naturally, groups of this size were impossible given the rigid confines of a four-wall handball court.

But when the troops returned to American shores or were discharged from their stateside stations, they had a new game which could be played almost anywhere with less wear-and-tear on the hands than handball, but involving the same amount of action and exercise.

Thus the paddleball boom was born, vastly expanding the field of competitive players and leading to the development of the national open tournaments in the early 1960's. However, the primary beneficiary of this boom was the one-wall game which, prior to the war, had been almost unknown. The current indications are that the one-wall game will continue to grow and probably outlast its four-wall ancestor in terms of general popularity.

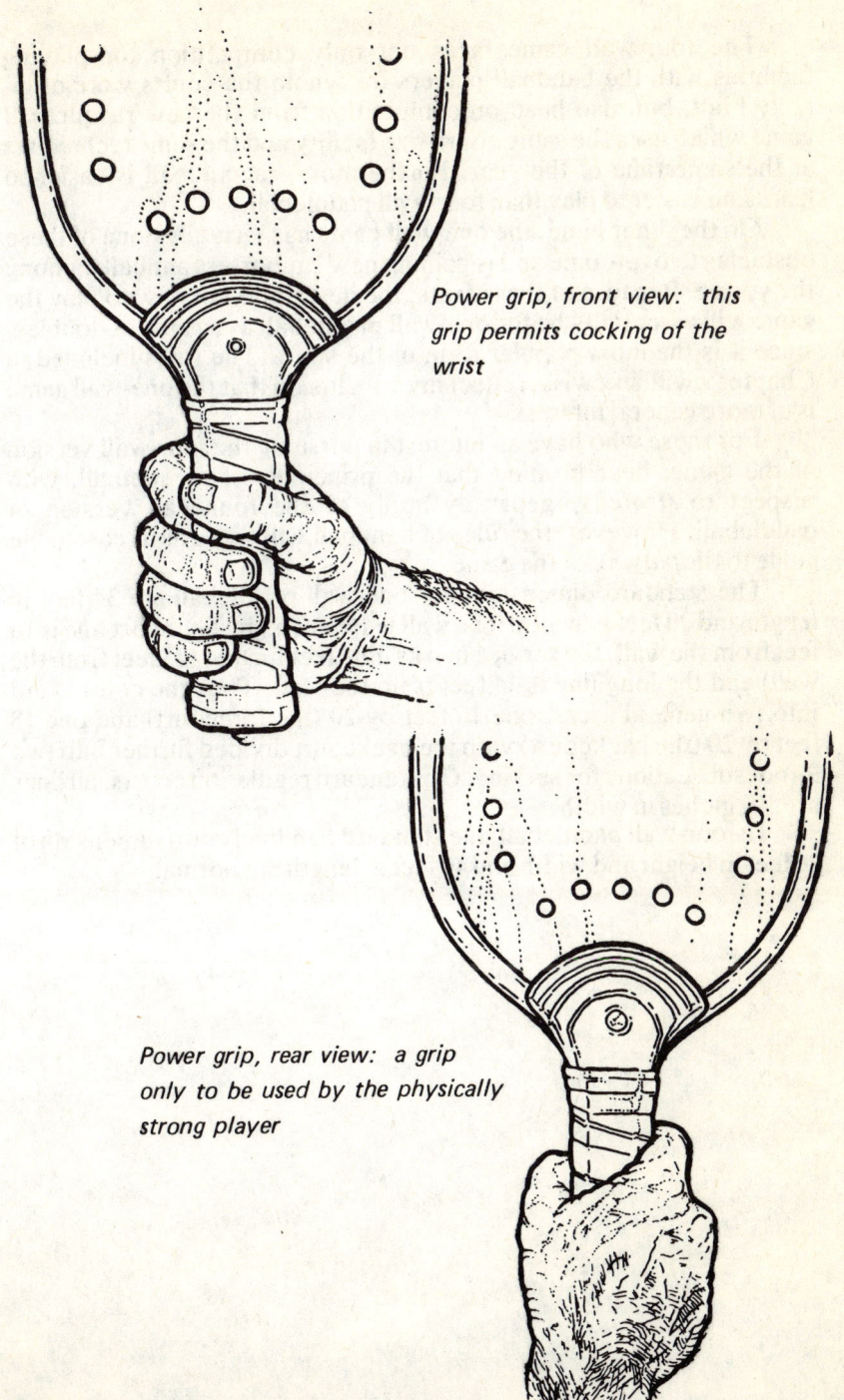

Power grip, front view: this grip permits cocking of the wrist

Power grip, rear view: a grip only to be used by the physically strong player

The four-wall game faces not only competition for playing facilities with the handball players for whom the courts were originally built, but also head-on competition from the new racquetball game which uses the same court-size facility and the same techniques at the same time of the year. Furthermore, racquetball is easier to learn and easier to play than four-wall paddleball.

On the other hand, the one-wall game has virtually none of these obstacles to overcome and is gaining new supporters annually among the young. Because of these facts, the description of how to play the game will essentially be for one-wall paddleball as a game of doubles, since it is the most popular form of the sport. The rules included in Chapter 9 will, likewise, reflect my conclusion that the one-wall game is of more general interest.

For those who have an interest in pursuing the four-wall version of the game, bear in mind that the principles of racquetball, with respect to *strategy,* generally apply to the four-wall version of paddleball. However, the rules of handball will serve as a reasonable guide to the *playing* of the game.

The standard dimensions for one-wall paddleball are 34 feet in length and 20 feet in width. The wall is 16 feet high. The short line is 16 feet from the wall, the service marks nine feet further (25 feet from the wall) and the long line is 34 feet from the wall. Thus the court is cut into two general areas, one 16 feet by 20 (the forecourt) and one 18 feet by 20 (the backcourt) with the backcourt divided further into two 9-foot subsections for serving. On standard regulation courts, all lines are 1½ inches in width.

In four-wall paddleball, the standard handball court dimension of 20 feet in height and width and 40 feet in length are normal.

chapter 6

How to Play Paddleball

THE FIRST STEP in getting a grip on how to play paddleball is to get a grip on the paddle. This can be done in any one of three or four different ways. For the neophyte, the so-called "choke grip" is generally recommended. It permits the greatest control of the paddle which is, of course, the first paramount consideration. In this grip, the paddle is pressed down as far as possible into the hand so that the thumb and forefinger are extended against the base of the paddle above the handle and the other three fingers are wrapped around the handle.

Some players have a habit of extending the forefinger along the side of the paddle or holding it straight forward into the surface of the paddle. These grips may, at first, give the impression of providing greater control but they do not and they will inhibit the player's maneuverability and tactics. These habits should be avoided. The forefinger should stretch across the base of the paddle not along its side or onto the striking surface.

The other optional grips are the standard grip in which the paddle is held much in the manner of a tennis racquet with the thumb and forefinger touching around the top of the handle and the so-called "power grip" in which the thumb and forefinger bisect the handle and all of the fingers close around the handle in a fist-like fashion.

The power grip works effectively only with the man with exceptional strength and who can defeat his opponents with power alone. This style eliminates most of the finesse from the game and is limiting with respect to strategy. Unless you have unusual upper-body and arm strength this grip is not recommended.

The service presents a variety of options and they are partially limited by the choice of grip. In standard singles play, the majority of the serves are either underhand or sidearm. In singles play, the sidearm serves have the extra dimension of enabling the server to mask the direction of his serve until the last moment and the ball is often in flight before the opponent can pick it up. In doubles, the overhand service is most often used, although both the sidearm and underhand may be used effectively and a mixture of the three is more effective still.

The power grip gives much more force to the overhand serve. The standard grips allow greater flexibility with the sidearm and underhand serves. The disadvantage to the choke grip is that it minimizes the wrist-snapping action and, therefore, takes away snap from the serve. Once you have enough confidence in your play to use the standard grip, it will open up greater tactical possibilities in your game.

The overhead service is the most workable since it permits the server to follow the flight of the ball (it moves away from him at eye-level) and also allows any player to develop a strong serve since leverage can be generated by the natural flow of the body weight from the rear to the front. Thus, raw strength is not a key factor in getting drive into an overhand service.

In all serves, the ball is struck off a bounce. Three bounces without a hit result in a fault and loss of point.

Normally, the feet should be parallel and the weight of the body evenly distributed on the serve. The weight shifts to the rear foot and the front foot raises slightly off the court when the ball is up. When the ball reaches the peak of its bounce, the arm is brought forward and the body weight shifts to the front foot as the paddle makes contact with the ball. A normal forward movement on the follow-through will place the server in position for his play of a return. The important aspect at this point is keeping your eye on the ball and positioning your feet to prepare for the return of service.

Always plan the placement of the service before bouncing the ball. Try to analyze the opponent's weaknesses and his previous response to service. Also you must be totally sure of the type of service you plan and the grip you will employ. There is no reason or excuse for indecision in this area once you have bounced the ball, but it is a malady among beginning players. Simply decide among the available options what you are going to do and do it. Even if it is the wrong choice it is superior to dropping a point on a fault or badly striking a service which may result in giving your opponent an easy point. Since only the serving team can score, you should be generally aggressive with the service and play out the point positively even if you selected the kind of serve incorrectly.

Forehand swing, using the choke grip

Forehand swing, using the Eastern grip

A poorly struck serve will loop instead of driving straight to the chosen area of the wall (which is normally about 12 feet up). A looping service gives the opponents more opportunity to plan and play their return and also increases the chances of the ball rebounding over the long line, a fault.

In addition to the normal service in the style of tennis, there is a no-step service in paddleball. In this instance, the server stands parallel to the wall and strikes the ball (either the sidearm or underhand serve) with the pivot of his body, shifting the weight forward and then turning to face the wall and prepare for the return.

An underhand serve is ideally struck about calf level and the sidearm service should made contact at waist level.

The basic strokes of the game are the forehand and backhand. With the standard grip, the forehand can be executed with a relatively short swing, longer than with the choke grip, but in either case the basic elements are the same. The ball is hit after a short backswing brings the paddle back slightly past the hip, the hip pivots and the weight shifts forward as the paddle comes forward and hits the ball slightly in front of the body. If more power is desirable for a given shot, the backswing can be extended back to the point in which the arm is straight out behind the body and parallel with the court. With the choke grip, the snap of the wrist is eliminated which cuts down one potential for a mechanical error and a misplay. With the standard grip, the wrist snap is at the point of impact with the ball and gives additional power to the shot.

On the backhand, as in all strokes, the control of the face of the paddle is important. Many shots are lost because of careless gripping of the paddle which permits the face to close against the wall. The face of the paddle should always be fully open (flat and parallel) in relation to the wall. A backhand is executed with the paddle in control, reaching across the body with a slight break in elbow and a natural snap-back motion, striking the ball slightly ahead of the body, pivoting the hips on the follow-through and shifting the weight from the back foot to the front.

At the point of impact on both the forehand and the backhand, the wrist should be uncocked and forming a straight line with the forearm and the elbow should also be straight so that it would be possible to draw a straight line from the paddle to the shoulder. The wrist should never be snapped after a shot or during a follow-through. This will cause a complete loss of control of the shot.

For those seeking to add additional power to the backhand there are two acceptable methods. One is by slightly looping or arcing the

Forehand swing, using the power grip

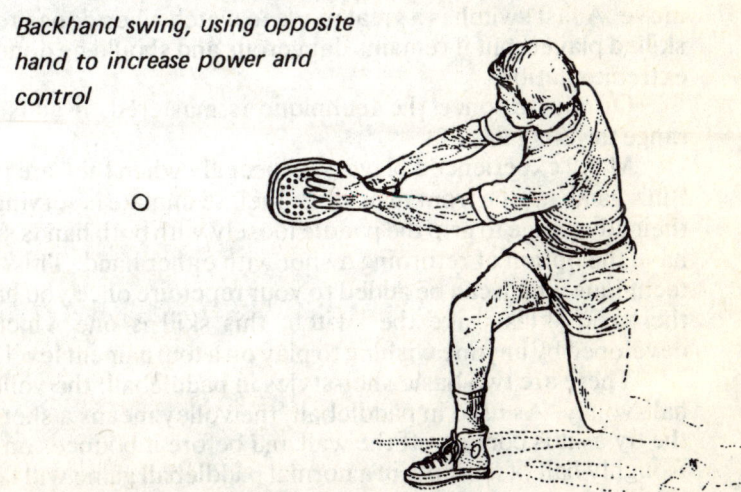

Backhand swing, using opposite hand to increase power and control

arm going into the swing and the other is by placing the opposite hand behind the paddle near the expected area of impact. Both of these methods will take some time to develop but they are worth the effort in expanding your arsenal of shots. Skillful players develop both techniques since each has optimum areas of application. On shots close to the body, the loop is preferable. On balls which must be hit away from the body and therefore some extension is required, the opposite hand style can be employed effectively.

One of the points upon which the National Association and the two Eastern groups are decidedly divided is the technique of switching hands with the paddle. In four-wall games common in the Midwest, a thong is attached to the paddle and the player must play all shots with the paddle on that hand. In the East, however, both the U.S. and American associations permit players to transfer the paddle from one hand to another to make particular shots.

However, this technique si not without its dangerous aspects as is obvious. Therefore, when first beginning to play one-wall it is strongly advised that the player always play with the paddle in one hand. If you are able to play with more experienced players, ask their advice when you are contemplating attempting to switch the paddle from one hand to the other. There is a temptation to do this very early on since it makes certain shots seem much easier. However, a backhand should be developed in any case since in higher class competition some shots will be taken so fast that switching is not a possibility. Also, an inexperienced player who is trying to switch can cause injury to himself and the other players if he is not capable of executing this move. A fast switch is a great move to watch when done properly by a skilled player, but it remains dangerous and should be done only with extreme caution.

Of course, once the technique is mastered, it adds still more range to your game.

Many experienced players, especially when they are playing the "in" game (as the front man while their teammate is serving) find it to their advantage to grip the paddle loosely with both hands so that they have the option of returning a shot with either hand. This, again, is a technique which can be added to your repetoire once you have gained the basic skills. Like the switch, this skill is one which must be developed by anyone wishing to play on a tournament level.

There are two basic shot-styles in paddleball: the volley and the half-volley. As used in paddleball, the volley means a shot played on the fly as it is coming off the wall and before it bounces on the court. Roughly half of all shots in a normal paddleball game will fall into this category.

The principal trick to the volley is to have the paddle ready to strike the ball as soon as it comes off the wall. In order to do this, you must determine where the point of impact is going to take place. Then you must decide what direction you want to give your returning shot. Naturally, when you are playing in the forecourt, you will hit the ball with a shorter stroke than when in the backcourt. But the impact of the ball off the wall will be greater so that the return velocity is generally about equal.

Clearly, some volleys are more difficult to hit than others. The most challenging is one which comes off the wall directly at your chest or face. The most effective way of returning this shot is simply by holding the paddle firmly between your body and the ball, to all intents and purposes letting it bounce off the paddle. This is called a "lift shot".

Since there is no backswing, wrist action or follow-through on a shot of this sort, it will not score many points for you. But it keeps the ball in play and permits you to get set for the next shot. The lift shot is, of course, a purely defensive shot. It can be made a little more effective if you turn your body so that you are almost perpendicular to the wall and give a chop stroke from the side. Footwork and agility are the key to this type of shot and it is risky because you may not be able to get the paddle up quickly enough to intercept the ball before it is past your body.

The half-volley is a ball which is played on just after it bounces. The ideal way to half-volley is to hit the ball as quickly after it strikes the court as possible. The shorter the bounce, the better your half-volley will be. Unlike some other racquet games strokes, a half-volley is a fairly effective shot in paddleball. Ideally, the ball should be hit when it is 6 inches or less from the court on the bounce, the paddle is pointed straight down and the follow-through is approximately parallel to the court. This shot is generally hit from a crouching position with the knees bent and the body leaning forward from the hips.

There is always a temptation to play the ball on a higher bounce since it seems easier. It may be easier, but it is not effective. No good players seek to play a ball on a high bounce. The ball should always be hit as close to the playing surface as possible. Of course, there will be many situations where the high bounce will be the only possible play, but this should never be your preference.

In common with other similar games, paddleball has overheads and lobs. However, they are somewhat different in their execution from other racquet and paddle sports. The overheads come in a variety of shapes and sizes. Interestingly, the overheads are now no longer considered normal paddleball shots since most players do not

The switch makes it possible to always use the forehand,

for most players their most powerful and controlled shot

Executing the overhead shot

The opposite hand, or switch

execute them correctly. The overhead smash is very nearly like the serve in tennis. The other overhead shots are the lob, drop and drive.

The most normal misplay of the overhead is to reach straight up and strike the ball with virtually no backswing. This is a sure way to lose points. The overhead should be executed with a backswing starting from the knee. With the paddle dropped to a line even with the knee and a slight bend in the elbow, the paddle is held at a right angle to the court. Your free arm is raised almost as though you are pointing at the on-coming ball.

The basic overhead movement is with the shoulder bringing the paddle arm up and over the head as the free arm swings down. The weight is on the ball of the back foot almost until the point of impact which should be either directly over or slightly behind the head. At the instant of contact, the back foot pushes off, shifting the weight forward.

The various overhead shots are distinguished in the following ways:

The drive - the paddle face must be parallel to the wall at the moment of impact and on the follow-through. This stroke aims the ball about seven or eight feet up on the wall. The drive is a good offensive weapon, especially when you believe the opponents are anticipating a soft lob return.

The lob - the face of the paddle must be angled upward toward the area of the wall at least 10 feet above the court, the higher the better and this angle must be retained on the follow-through. This is a difficult shot to properly execute but is a very valuable tool to prevent the opposition from making a quick shot for a point and also allowing time for you to get set for the next return. The arm is brought forward in the normal overhead motion but with less force than in the drive.

The drop - the wrist is the key to this shot, probably one of the game's most difficult to execute correctly. Much practice will be required to master the overhead drop, but it is perhaps the most deft and beautiful maneuver the game has to offer. When the arm is brought over the head, the wrist is turned downward slightly at the moment of impact with the ball, directing the shot toward the lower portion of the wall and the follow-through is shortened to soften the shot. When properly done, this shot will hit the wall in one of the corners about two feet above the court surface and drop softly for a sure point.

The smash - this is not really an overhead shot but rather, as previously mentioned, it follows the form of the tennis serve. The paddle passes directly over the shoulder rather than the head, but the balance and weight shifting principles are the same. The smash is particularly useful when the ball is coming off the high part of the wall and is heading toward the upper part of your body or over your head. A slight backward bend of the body will line up the ball, the arm is then brought back so that the elbow is slightly further back than the shoulder, the wrist is dropped back from the forearm which is angled slightly backward. The weight is transferred to the back foot, the swing is made when the arm comes forward away from the body and the arm is fully extended at the moment of impact. The follow-through is important. It should come over the shoulder down toward the knee with the wrist twisting to keep the paddle face parallel with the surface of the court. As effective as this shot is, it is not one which the normal player will find frequently used.

From the standpoint of strategy, there are a few basic points which all players must keep in mind. Foremost, of course, is the general ability of the players involved. Assuming a doubles match, the best player on your team should always play the left side if both are righthanded. In the event he is lefthanded, he should play the right side.

Your partner is the key to your success in paddleball doubles, regardless of his ability.

Don't use him as an excuse for mistakes. A good working relationship with your partner will make paddleball a much more rewarding experience for both of you. If you have the superior ability, try to take on as much of the load as you can handle, but don't try to play the entire game yourself. Give your partner as much as he can handle, too.

Don't put your partner in an impossible position, if it can at all be avoided. For example, if he is behind his man, make his opponent move for the ball if possible and open up your man.

Perhaps most important of all, talk to your partner continuously during the match. Paddleball is a quick-paced game in which changing of positions will be occurring throughout the match. Keep your partner posted on what you are doing. He can't be expected to watch you and play his man, keep his eyes on the ball and plan his own shots all at once. But he can certainly hear you and make it your business to be sure he does.

Generally, yell "got it" or just "got" when you have a return which you can play, no matter which side of your body the ball is on. Always yell when you are going to return a ball so that your partner doesn't collide with you trying to make a shot on the same ball; or, worse yet, you both let a ball pass assuming the other man is going to take it. Never assume in paddleball.

When you cross the court to make a shot, yell "switch" so that your partner knows he must cover the area which you just vacated. This, of course, is especially important if your partner is playing the "in" game, but call it anyway even if you are the front man.

If, in your opinion, a ball going over your head (and, possibly, your partner's) is out, call "out". Don't be bashful about calling "out". Of course, once in a great while we all make mistakes and the ball may be in, but your judgment will rapidly improve on these calls. In any event, the mere fact that you call "out" makes your partner aware of the possibility. Even if he has the superior ability and experience, he may not at that second be conscious of his precise position on the court and your call will make his mind focus on the possibility or probability of the play going out. If he doesn't share your judgment, he will go for the ball anyway. In either case, call what you think it is.

Paddleball, like handball and racquetball, involves a good deal of movement forward, backward and from one side of the court to the other. This will involve body contact and "crowding." Some players are very skillful at a deliberate crowd and, frankly, this is part of the game. However, the rules will protect you from obvious blocks and interference by your opponents. In these cases, a "hinder" is called. In tournament play, referees and, sometimes, linesmen are provided to make the calls. Clearly, in schoolyard and informal games, you will make your own calls.

When you feel you have been hindered, call it immediately, but make every effort to make the shot anyway. The referee (or your opponents) may not agree with you. After you have played the game for awhile, you will get accustomed to the local interpretations for hinders. This will let you know what you can do and what you can expect from the opposition. But paddleball is designed so that the body contact is incidental, not an integral, part of the game and you should not make a practice of overtly hindering the opposition. However, intent is not really an issue in a hinder. Even if the hinder is unintentional, it will be called either for you or against you.

In the meantime, get yourself a paddle, hurry right over to the nearest park and begin enjoying paddleball. It is a game which will give you great satisfaction and help you maintain good physical condition, improve your stamina and your muscle tone.

chapter 7

Platform Tennis

THE GAME OF PLATFORM TENNIS was developed by two men in Westchester County, New York, somewhat by happenstance. The pair, Fessenden S. Blanchard and James K. Cogswell, were avid tennis enthusiasts who were seeking some way of maintaining their physical activity during the winter months when it was impractical to play tennis in the northeastern United States due to the weather conditions.

As an outgrowth of their many conversations on this problem, Cogswell decided to build a raised platform on his property in Scarsdale, New York, upon which they thought a variety of games might be played during the winter months. Among the games they thought of were volleyball, deck tennis, ping pong and badminton.

The first platform was constructed in late 1928 and was enclosed with a wire to keep errant shots from rolling away into the snow or landing on the road near Cogswell's property. However, once the platform was completed, the two friends discovered that playing the games they had planned on simply didn't work on the platform.

Therefore, Cogswell decided to figure out some type of recreational game which would provide sufficient activity to maintain body warmth, enough interest to sustain a sense of competition *and* work on an enclosed platform. He ended up by buying some paddle ball racquets and balls from a local sporting goods store and platform tennis was on its way.

In league with Blanchard, Cogswell developed the new sport using the tools of a game of paddle tennis which was then played with some regularity in playgrounds in nearby New York City. The equipment was simple enough for the city kids and their parents to buy and easy to store. It consisted of small rubber balls and short-handle paddles, similar to, but slightly larger than, today's table tennis paddles. Paddle tennis had also been played in schools and gymnasiums, but was not a regular varsity sport.

With their already-constructed platform and using most of the rules of tennis, Blanchard and Cogswell started off. They used two serves, as in standard tennis and after having hit a few balls, they made some adjustments to the rules which adapted the game to its enclosure and created platform tennis.

Availability of land has restricted the size of the platform to roughly 48 feet in length and 20 feet in width. In their initial efforts, Blanchard and Cogswell used the measurements for the standard paddle tennis court, 39 feet by 18 feet, roughly half the standard tennis court dimensions. They adjusted this to the size of a badminton court, 44 feet by 20 feet. Since this change almost filled the entire area they had built, they allowed shots which struck the wire and bounced once in the court to be played, thus making the wire enclosure an integral part of the game.

This stroke of creative thinking made platform tennis the exciting and challenging game it is today. The rebounds off the wire are the most difficult and interesting aspect of platform tennis, an aspect which will be more fully discussed in the next chapter.

Blanchard and Cogswell also learned a couple of other things which were crucial to the development of the game. First, that a strong service could handcuff the opposing player, especially if the first service was in play. Therefore, they eliminated the second service to take the edge off the power serve. With only one serve permitted, the stress is naturally on accuracy rather than power in the serve. They also found that the newly-restructured game was more adaptable to doubles play than singles, although singles was contested for several years on a tournament level and can, of course, still be played if only two players are available.

What the men had wrought at this point was a game which has changed but little in the intervening decades. One principal innovation was made a few years later, however, when Donald K. Evans developed what is now the standard backstop to curb the often totally erratic bounces off the wire which were a common problem in the early days of the game. With this development, the court was enlarged slightly to its now standard dimensions of 61 feet by 31 feet and the back and side wire was raised to 12 feet in height.

The name, too, was changed rather quickly.

Originally, the sport was known as paddle tennis because it was an outgrowth of that game. In certain sections of many Eastern areas it is still called, informally, "paddle." However, Blanchard and Cogswell named it platform paddle tennis to distinguish it from its cousin. The game is now formally known as platform tennis and is supervised by the American Platform Tennis Association based at the Fox Meadow Tennis Club in Scarsdale, New York.

Platform tennis became a social rage in Westchester and Southern New England in the late 1920's and by the early 1930's platforms had been built through the area including such places as Rye, Cedarhurst, Larchmont, New Haven, Springfield, and on Martha's Vineyard. In the fall of 1931, Fox Meadow became the first large country club to build a platform for the game, all of the previous platforms having been built for private use. Within three years, several other major country clubs, which had principally been interested in golf and tennis, joined in the construction of platform tennis courts in the Northeast. A major jump came in 1934 with the organization of the American Platform Tennis Association.

In 1935, the A.P.T.A. organized national championship tournaments in five categories: men's singles and doubles, women's singles and doubles and mixed doubles. Since that time, other categories have been added, including senior (over-50) men's doubles in 1957 and boys doubles in 1963. The singles competitions were dropped after 1937.

Blanchard was the first president of the A.P.T.A. and served in that capacity until 1938. During its early years, platform tennis remained something of a local popular sport in southern New York and New England. It really didn't begin to gain what one could charitably call widespread popularity until after World War II. While the area of its birth is still the citadel of the game, platform tennis now has enthusiasts throughout North America.

In the first national tournament for men at Fox Meadow, 22 doubles teams were entered, representing clubs from Greenwich, South Orange, Rye, New Rochelle and Hartsdale, as well as Scarsdale. In recent years, the number both of teams and clubs represented has grown impressively. Not surprisingly, Scarsdale teams won both the men's and women's national titles in the 1935 championship. In the men's finals on February 24, 1935, Clifford D. Couch and Sumner D. Kilmarx won the men's title by defeating Charles O'Hearn and James N. Hynson in the final, 4-6, 6-4, 6-3, 2-6 and 9-7 in an exciting match which did a good deal to promote the popularity of the game. The women's final had been held two days earlier at the Manursing Island Club in Rye, New York, with Mrs.

Percy Fuller and Mrs. Henry Eaton of Scarsdale sweeping past Mrs. Godfrey Rockefeller and Mrs. Foster Hampton of Greenwich, 6-1, 6-1.

Hynson, though beaten in the first final, was one of the game's early evangelists and was among the driving forces behind Fox Meadow's original construction of a platform in 1931. Today, Fox Meadow has nine platforms, more than any other club in America.

In 1935, the singles titles were won by C. E. Grafmueller who beat Dick Newell, 6-1, 6-2, 6-2, for the men's championship. Mrs. Henry B. Eaton captured the women's crown with a 6-4, 6-3 win over Mrs. Edward Raymond, Sr. The mixed doubles final saw Charles O'Hearn and Mrs. Fuller team to defeat Mr. and Mrs. Couch, 6-4, 4-6, 6-3.

Absent from among the list of the female finalists was Mrs. T. Edmund Beck who was to dominate the game on the distaff side for most of the next twenty-five years. She won her first doubles title in 1938 with Mrs. C.H. Walker as a partner. This tandem was to win every women's doubles national championship from 1938 to 1942, after which competition was suspended because of World War II. Tournament began again in 1949.

That year, Mrs. Beck was back. Now paired with a former rival, Mrs. Oscar F. Moore, Mrs. Beck won the 1949 title, finished second in the 1950 tournament, and, still playing with Mrs. Moore, she won the crown in 1951, 1952, 1953 and 1954. Virtually any team of which she was a member became a championship contender. In 1955 and 1956, Mrs. Beck finished second in the women's doubles championships playing with a different partner each year. After failing to make the final in 1957 for the first time in 20 years, she returned as a champion in 1959 and 1960. This time she had the unique experience of playing in and winning the national title with her daughter, Susan (Mrs. William Wasch). In 1939, she had won the national mixed doubles title with her husband and the Becks had finished second in the mixed finals in 1940 and 1941.

After World War II, the number of championship husband-and-wife teams playing in mixed doubles began to decline. Mrs. Beck reached the finals in 1950 and 1952 with two different partners, but lost both times. In 1953, she paired up with Richard K. Hebard and won the title by defeating Mr. and Mrs. Ronald Carroll, the last of the powerful husband-and-wife teams. The Carrolls had won the mixed title four straight years from 1949 to 1952, but no team of married partners has won it since.

(Photo Credit: Tribuno Wines, Inc., Sponsors of the Tribuno Platform Tennis Circuit.)

With Hebard as a partner, Mrs. Beck won the championship in 1954 and 1956, finishing second in 1955. The 1956 crown was her last in mixed competition and in 1957, Hebard teamed with Ruth Chalmers to win the title. Oddly, the team Hebard and Miss Chalmers beat in the finale was James Carlisle and Susan Beck.

Upon Mrs. Beck's Retirement from the scene, her place was almost immediately taken by Mrs. S. Warren Lee who became the dominant player in women's competition. In 1961, Mrs. Lee was on the winning teams in both the mixed doubles and women's doubles in the national championships. She and her partner, James P. Gordon, also won the mixed title in 1962 and Mrs. Lee was a part of the mixed championship combination for the third successive year in 1963 when she paired with Hebard, giving him the distinction of playing with probably the two finest women players in the history of platform tennis.

Mrs. Lee was also on the winning side in the mixed play in 1965 and 1969, finishing second in 1964, 1966, 1967, 1968 and 1970. In women's doubles, Mrs. Lee's record was, if possible, even more impressive. She succeeded Mrs. Beck in 1961 with Mrs. Charles Sager as a partner. After failing to make the finals in 1962, she was on the winning team in 1963 and 1964, the runner-up team in 1965, and was a part of the championship combination in 1966 (with Mrs. Edgar Nelson), 1967, 1968, 1969 and 1970 (with Mrs. Charles Stanton) and was rapidly closing in on the records held by Mrs. Beck who had won a total of seventeen national titles (12 in women's doubles, four in mixed doubles and one in women's singles). With her 1970 triumph, Mrs. Lee matched Mrs. Beck's record of being part of the women's doubles championship team for five successive years.

Considered one of the top tactical players in the game, Mrs. Lee, in 1966 was one of the first women ever to win the Honor Award of the A.P.T.A. while still an active player. Another outstanding woman player was Mrs. Mary Adair Moore a winning partner in the national women's doubles in 1937, 1949, 1951, 1952, 1953 and 1954 and the mixed doubles in 1946.

Although he was on the losing side during that first national doubles final in 1935, Charles O'Hearn became the dominant male player in the sport until the early 1950's. He was on the men's doubles winners in 1937, 1938, 1943 and 1948 and played on the runner-up team in the doubles, in addition to the 1935 inaugural, in 1939, 1945, 1946 and 1949. He also teamed with his wife to win the national mixed doubles crown four times (1936, 1937, 1938 and 1940). He had won the

(Photo Credit: Tribuno Wines, Inc., Sponsors of the Tribuno Platform Tennis Circuit.)

first mixed doubles with Mrs. Percy Fuller in 1935. O'Hearn was also the last national singles winner in 1937, defeating Richard Newell, 6-0, 6-2, 6-3.

In recent years, other players have come to prominence, including Bradley Drowne and Gordon Gray, who were two of the top men players in the 1960's. Gray won the mixed doubles with Mrs. William G. Symmers in 1966, 1967 and 1968, while teaming with Jesse Sammis III to win the men's doubles in 1969 and 1970. Drowne was Mrs. Lee's partner in the 1969 and 1970 mixed doubles finals. The team won the crown in 1969 and was beaten in the finals, 6-2, 7-5, by John Mangan and Sue Harris the following year. Mangan and Chauncey Steele were among the top players in the early 1970's.

Over the years, the popularity of the game has spread away from the counties clustered around New York City which had given it birth and nurtured it in its early years. Courts now span the northern half of the country going as far south as Virginia, Maryland and Washington, D.C., and extending across the country from Toronto to California. Bowling Green University in Ohio has an outstanding 4-platform complex on its campus and several other colleges also have platforms.

Many clubs devoted to the playing of tennis have constructed platform tennis installations as well, with the rising interest in the game including the prestigious West Side Tennis Club in Forest Hills, long the home of the U.S. Open Tennis championships and its forerunners. The West Side was, in fact, the host of the 1976 national men's and women's doubles championships of the A.P.T.A.

Along the way to its current high level of popularity, platform tennis has had, naturally, many boosters who were active in promoting the game since its creation by Cogswell and Blanchard (neither of whom ever won a national championship, incidentally, although Blanchard played on a runner-up team in men's doubles in 1936).

Among those who have made distinguished contributions to the game without being championship players were the late Earle Gotchell and Harold D. Holmes, John A. Stephenson and George Harrison. Gotchell was particularly devoted to developing young players and today the national boys' doubles trophy is dedicated to his memory. Holmes helped spread the gospel of platform tennis into New Jersey in its early days, while Stephenson was a major devotee to night play and played many exhibitions under the lights to popularize the idea. This was a great help in making the game a year-round recreation. It was partly because of night play that Harri-

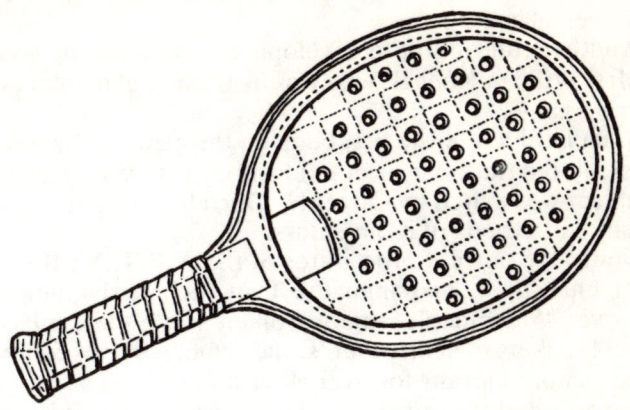

Two racquets, the leather wrist thong is optional

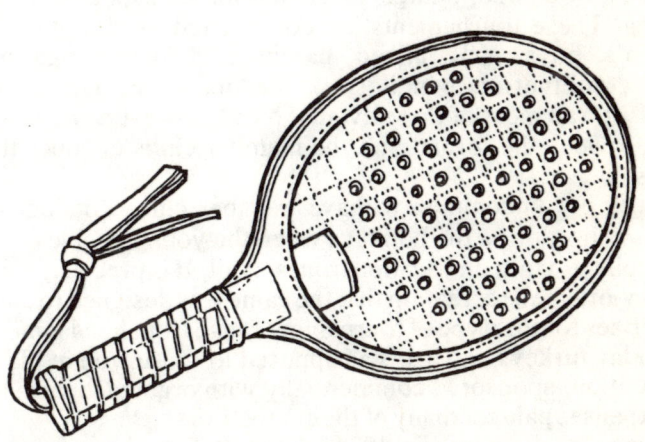

son was instrumental in developing the yellow-orange ball which is now universal in the game.

Another contributor to developing interest among young people was Mrs. William Koegel, who was instrumental in interesting many girls in the game.

Blanchard wrote the first book on the game and worked hard to promote it, but the most successful and currently authorized work on the subject was edited by Oliver H. Durrell, a long-time exponent of the game and a friend of its inventors.

Under the current procedures of the A.P.T.A., there are eight tournaments sanctioned annually. They include the national men's, men's over 45, women's, senior women's, boys and mixed doubles and two brackets of senior men's, the senior for over 50 years of age and the senior veterans for over 60 years of age. The two classes of senior men's and the mixed doubles are normally conducted in February, the men's and women's nationals in March and the boys in December.

As with any compact game, platform tennis lends itself to all manner of different tournaments. Areas where platforms are plentiful have seen infinite varieties. One of the first groups to be innovative was the Manursing Island Club in Rye which developed a "scrambles" or "jamble" tournament. Here, the players all enter as individuals and are matched on teams according to ability, pairing weaker players with stronger ones, to make a balance in the competition. There is, of course, a large social and family aspect to this kind of playing. These tournaments are constructed as invitational men's, women's, boys, girls, mixed, parent-child, member-guest or any other combination which suits the occasion. Until 1959, the A.P.T.A. ran most of these events. Now, however, the Association only provides the format and the member clubs conduct their own events.

It is not uncommon to have member clubs conduct platform tournaments during the holidays when the young people come home from college or are on vacation from school. It is precisely this type of socially-oriented recreation that the game was designed to create.

Prizes for this type of tournament range from handsome trophies to holiday turkeys and hams as opposed to those won in the national competition, sponsored commercially with ornate trophies the prize and expenses paid for many of the competitors.

Since its founding in 1934, the A.P.T.A. has grown into an organization with 50,000 nationwide members and its club and indi-

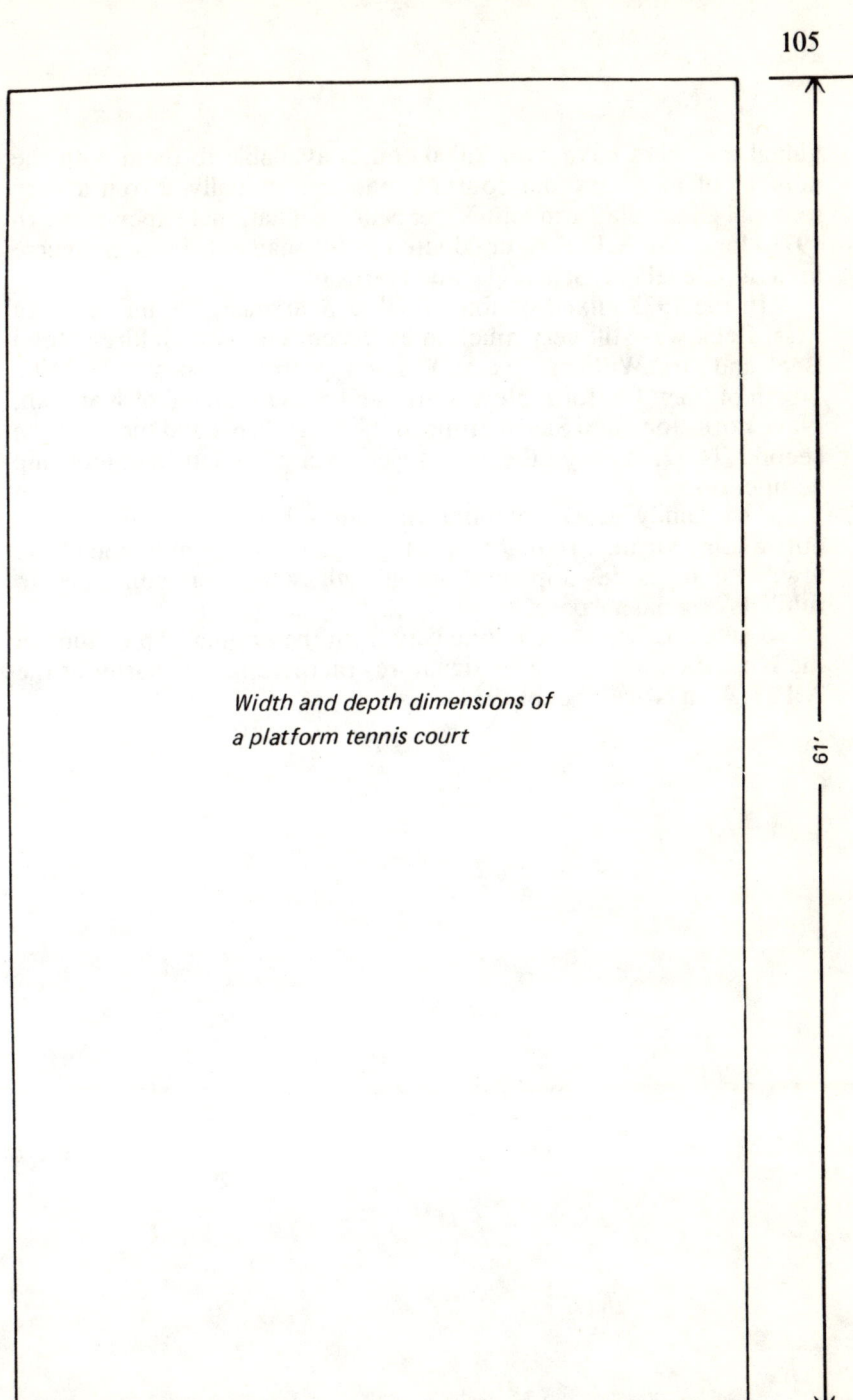
Width and depth dimensions of a platform tennis court

vidual members have over 2,000 courts available to them with the number of members and courts expanding annually. From a very regional game, platform tennis has become a national experience. In 1973 alone, the A.P.T.A. conducted its tournaments in such diverse areas as Cleveland, Scarsdale, and Hartford.

In the 1973 mixed doubles final at Scarsdale, the influence of Mrs. Beck was still very much in evidence. Her two children, John Beck and Mrs. William (Susan) Wasch were finalists, beaten by Mike North of New Bedford, New York, and Sis O'Connell of Katonah, New York. John and Susan dropped the first set, 6-1 and then lost the second, 14-12, in one of the longest sets ever played in championship competition.

The family aspect of platform tennis has become one of its outstanding virtues. In that respect, the game is probably one of the few, despite its development and growth, which has continued to fulfill its original purpose.

The game has come a long way from the original three clubs in the Northeast who put their signatures on the original charter of the A.P.T.A. in November of 1934.

chapter 8

How to Play Platform Tennis

THE BASIC APPROACH to playing platform tennis is the same as that to the game of tennis but the judgment factors of the game are substantially different.

Generally, the racquet is gripped the same way as it is in tennis. The service form is much the same and the good return rule is almost identical. From there, however, there start to be some significant differences. The major factor in platform tennis is, of course, the wire fence surrounding the court. Since balls off the wire are considered in play if they bounce only once and, in fact, constitute much of the action in the game, a discussion of how to play platform tennis centers around the wire.

One of the primary rules of platform tennis is that the server must always come to the net. Bear in mind that the game is basically one of doubles. Singles are played, but rarely, and as noted in the previous chapter, they have not been included in national championships since 1937.

Since the partner is already in the forecourt, the server coming to the net puts both teammates in the forecourt. This is something which would never happen in standard tennis as a matter of strategy, but it is vital in platform tennis. The reason is that there is much less concern about a ball being hit past a player in platform tennis. In fact, the best bet is to let anything go which even remotely appears to be going out. In the event that you have misjudged the ball and the shot is in play, you still have the opportunity to recover by playing it off the wire on the rebound.

Resist the temptation to smash a ball coming across the net, especially if you hit above mid-chest level. Odds are that the shot will go out. And, if it doesn't, there is always the wire.

Playing a ball off the wire is not as simple as it appears when skilled players do it. Players new to the game are often guilty of hitting a ball too soon when it comes off the wire or starting their motion too early. Balls come rather slowly off the wire and hitting them too early results in many lost points.

It should be noted at this stage that platform tennis is largely a game of errors. It is much more difficult to hit a clean winning shot in platform tennis than it is in standard tennis. At least half of all points scored in a normal platform tennis game, even between proficient players, are scored on errors by the opponent. If anything, this figure is a conservative one.

In tennis, only about 10 or 15% of all points are scored on errors. Judgment, therefore, is more important in platform tennis than, in a sense, is physical skill. Timing and awareness of the angles matter more than almost any physical attribute with the possible exception of stamina. Since the confines of the court cut down on the stroke, height and weight mean little. With the introduction of the perforated paddles and sanded surfaces, a wide variety of shots are now available to players of platform tennis. But skill in executing these shots can be wasted if discretion is not exercised in shot selection.

If you are the server, you go to net immediately after the service. Remember, accuracy is crucial in the service since the rules do not permit second service. Also, technique and care matter since one fault costs you a point.

When you go to net, go closely to the net. In tennis, it is normally recommended that a player stay four to six feet away from the net. In platform tennis, you get as close as you can without actually hitting the net. Few, if any, points in a normal match will be won in the background, but many effective shots can be made right at the net and skilled players are often only a matter of inches away from those shots most of the match—except when they have to chase balls off the wire.

The offensive team has a distinct advantage in this sense since they have one player already at net and the server has a natural follow-through to it.

If the return of service appears to be going out, let it go but be ready to break back toward the wire if your judgement is incorrect. Remember, when the ball hits the wire it will be slower coming off of it than you think and you will have time to play it. A little practice will give you a feel for the amount of time you will need to get to the wire to catch a rebound and play it.

The overhand serve is normally used, but some excellent players have perfected an underhand serve which is perfectly permissible.

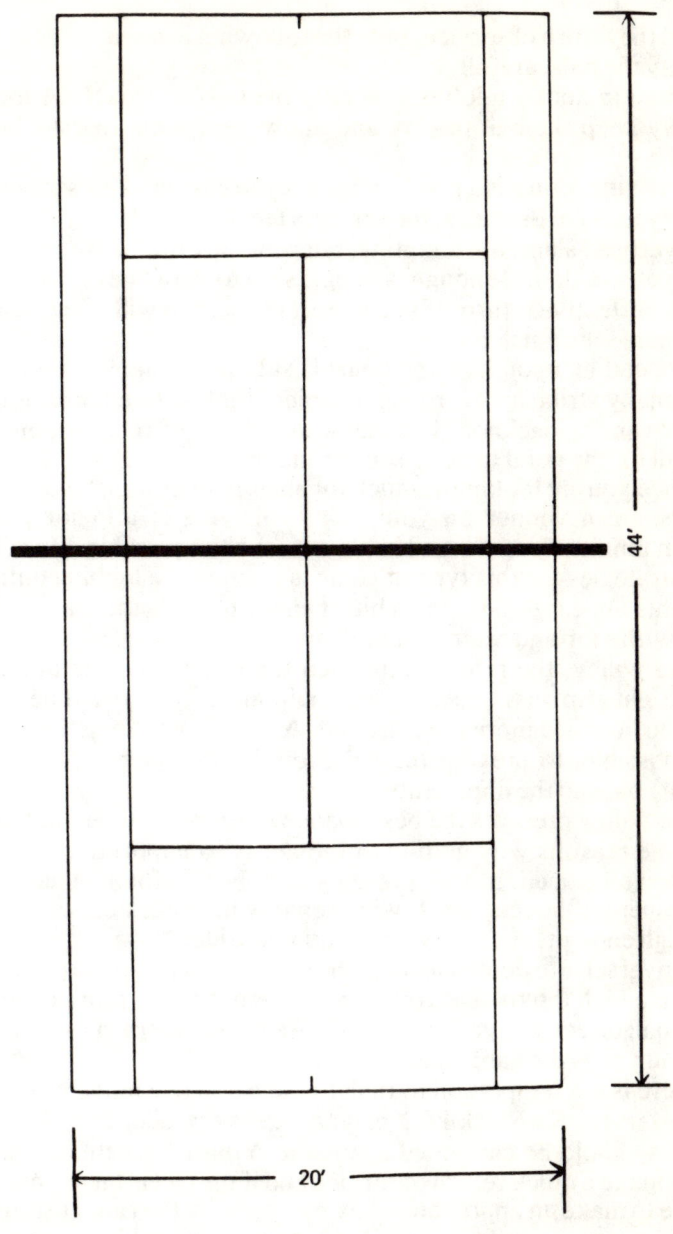

Complete diagram of the construction of a platform tennis court

On the return of service, bear the following in mind:
Play the ball carefully.

When in doubt, a lob is generally the best approach. A lob will normally keep the ball in play and allow your team to establish its rhythm.

A driving return is a good weapon if you can handle a service that way. Try to drive the ball at the server's feet if possible.

Overhead slams are tempting, but generally futile.

If you are skillful enough, an angle shot toward one of the corners is also an effective return. If you keep it in, the ball will often "die" in the corners for a quick point.

Depending upon how the court is situated, you may have a ball occasionally strike an overhanging object (lights, tree limbs, etc.) or bound over the backboard or sidewall. If any of this happens, the rules call for the point to be re-served and played over.

Since you are looking as much for an opponent's mistake and you are to score a winner on your side, volleying is a major part of platform tennis. Keep the ball in play as much as possible. One of the better strategies for this type of game is to continue lobbing until the opponents appear to be tiring a bit, then try to drive them away from the net with a lob and return with a drop shot.

In a volley, the return is handled the same way it is in tennis. Keep a tight grip on the racquet and maintain a stiff wrist. The volley should be punched more than stroked. Always try to keep the returns low if possible, to prevent the ball from hitting the backboard and bounding back to the opponents.

The volley presents the best chance to score a winner and this is one of the reasons why getting to the net is so important. If a drop volley is well placed, it, too, presents possibilities for a winner since the opponent, if he reaches it, will probably hit it back either into the net or high enough for an easy volley on your side.

Conversely, to defend against the drop volley, if you can reach it, throw up a high lob to give your team a chance to get reorganized or aim the ball directly at your opponent. As I said before, a ball coming directly at you is the hardest to return.

There is the temptation to rush to the net in one move when you are the server. Some skillful players are very adept at this, but beginners should be cautioned against it. Your opponents are quite likely to make a quick return of service and if the ball is hit to you, you will have to make an approach volley by hitting on the run. Hitting the ball on the move should be avoided whenever possible. Therefore, make as much of a move toward the net as possible, allowing time to

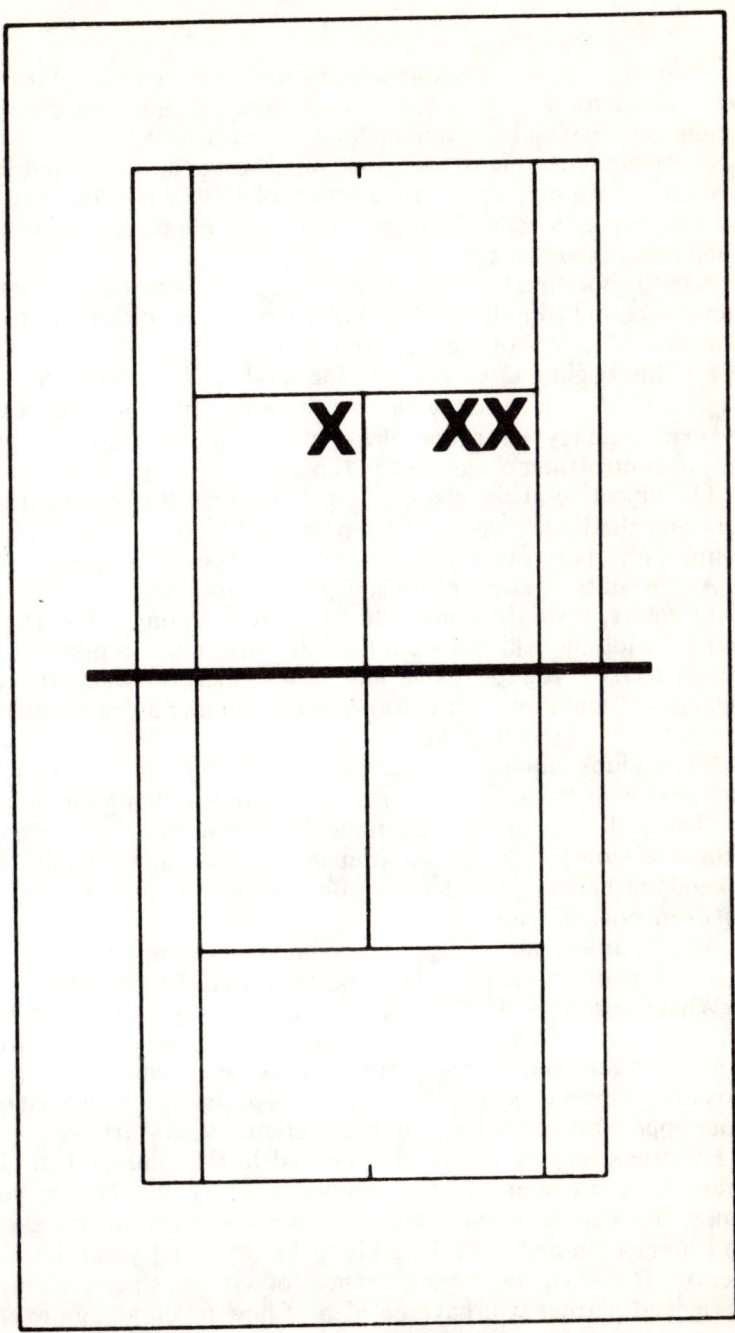

Illustration for serve into Ad and Deuce Courts

plant your feet for the possible approach volley. Once a return has been made into the opponent's court, quickly move as close as possible to the net and set yourself for the net volley.

If you are receiving service and you observe the server making a quick rush to the net, an effective return of service is a lob over the onrushing server's head. Unless you are very adept at it, smashing the ball is not good strategy.

A hard shot directly into one of the corners is perhaps the most difficult rebound to judge and will often carom erratically, but it is also a most difficult shot to execute correctly.

For the beginning player, the lob is always the best shot, although naturally the strategy calls for a variety of shots and as you grow in proficiency, your repetoire of shots will increase as will your ability to control their placement and speed.

The objective of the game is largely to force the opponent into errors and the longer you can keep the ball in play with the least amount of effort on your part, the more likely this is to happen.

At the outset, concentrate on getting your service into play without faults, since these are automatically lost points. Then try to continually lob the ball and keep the rally alive until an opportunity presents itself for you to strike a shot for a winner. It is likely that the opponent will make an error before you hit a winner if you are able to keep the ball consistently alive.

Many clubs employ a system in which the team that wins six points first wins the set, whether or not there is a two-point advantage. This is done to shorten the time of the matches when there is a shortage of courts and is common during the early rounds of a weekend tournament. This has the effect, of course, of making every point even more valuable.

Almost universally, except in the national championships, platform tennis matches are played on a best two-out-of-three set basis.

What most clubs do is match the weakest players with the best ones on a team. Therefore, you are likely to learn as much from playing with an experienced partner as you are from watching the opposition. This is especially true since it is probable that at least one of your opponents will have no more experience than you have.

Experienced players are accustomed to this situation in club "scramble" tournaments and you should make a point of telling your partner what degree of experience you possess at playing the game. Don't be bashful or boastful, tell him the truth and you'll both be better off. It also enhances your chances of winning since your more experienced partner will have an idea of how much he can expect from you and may make an effort to play balls, especially off the wire, which he would normally not play if he had a more experienced player on his team.

You will find experienced players can judge with startling accuracy the rebound of the ball off the wire. This will come to everyone after playing seriously and regularly. It is also important to avoid overplaying a ball so that you wind up backed against the wire or played into a corner where you can be of very little help to your partner, especially if the return goes to the opposite side of the court, a reasonable possibility if your opponents are alert. Try to maintain your balance when you run to get a ball near the wire. Don't charge it any more quickly than you must.

Platform tennis is an elemental game and the basic concepts follow many other games, such as tennis and badminton. But it has many little nuances of its own and if you follow the basic guidelines of sound play and work to avoid errors, the game will be very enjoyable.

To Sum Up:

Platform tennis possesses three unique characteristics: a small court, the 12 ft. high screen surrounding the court and the single serve. All three of these encourage long, exciting points wherein each team must try to outmaneuver the other, as in a master chess match.

The small size of the platform tennis court makes it easy to cover. A shot is seldom hit out of a player's reach. Thus, in order to win a point the other team must be constantly moved around the court until a real opening is developed. This tandem movement on the small court requires split second reaction so there must be constant communication (calls of *yours, mine, out, hit,* etc.).

The screened walls of the platform tennis court provide a *second chance*. If a ball is hit *through* a team, they may turn and play the shot as it rebounds off the wire. Putting the ball away with a power shot is very difficult.

The single serve in platform tennis puts a premium on accuracy, not power. There are very few service aces. Thus, the return of serve may become a powerful weapon.

These characteristics help to give platform tennis its special appeal and the shots in the game are all geared toward a common goal: to enable the team to gain the net position. In platform tennis the team that controls the net controls the game. Let's consider each shot so that you will know what to look for in a match.

The Serve

Since there is only one serve allowed, each player must determine how much pace and spin to put on the serve. Watch for the players who are daring enough to hit *the big serve*—although almost all will add some spin as a safety measure. Most top players will try to serve to specific spots in the service box. In the deuce court, most serves should be into the backhand corner. In the ad court, the server will try to *jam* the receiver. Obviously, varying the service spot will keep the receiver off balance.

The Return of Serve

Almost all service returns are hit as forehands in platform tennis. The adcourt player will *run around* the serve to hit a forehand return. The new crop of young players have made the service return a lethal weapon. Watch them follow their drive-returns to the net where they will attempt to volley for a winner. This is called *Blitzing*. There are several possible returns of serve: drive, lob, dink (a soft, sharply dropping shot) and a return off the screen. The drive will be hit cross court or down-the-line; the lob may go over the net player or cross court; the dink will drop over the center of the net or sharply cross court; the wire return will either be lobbed or driven.

Lob

The lob is one of the most frequently hit shots in platform tennis. It may be hit defensively or offensively. Defensive lobs are usually hit off the wire as a means of keeping the ball in play. This is a *holding* maneuver. Offensive lobs move the opposing team back from the net where they must either hit a weak overhead or play the ball on the bounce. Either way, the lobbing team may take over the key net position. Ideally, a lob should be hit over the opposing team's backhands or deep down the middle.

Overhead

Since the lob is one of the most frequently hit shots in platform tennis, it follows that lots of overheads will set up for the opposition. On fairly deep lobs, the safest overhead to hit would be one into the middle of the court (nearer to the deuce court player's backhand) or into the ad court corner.

On a short lob, the overhead may be hit down more sharply into the court so that it will *die* on the screen. There are several target areas: the back screen near the corners, the side screen near the

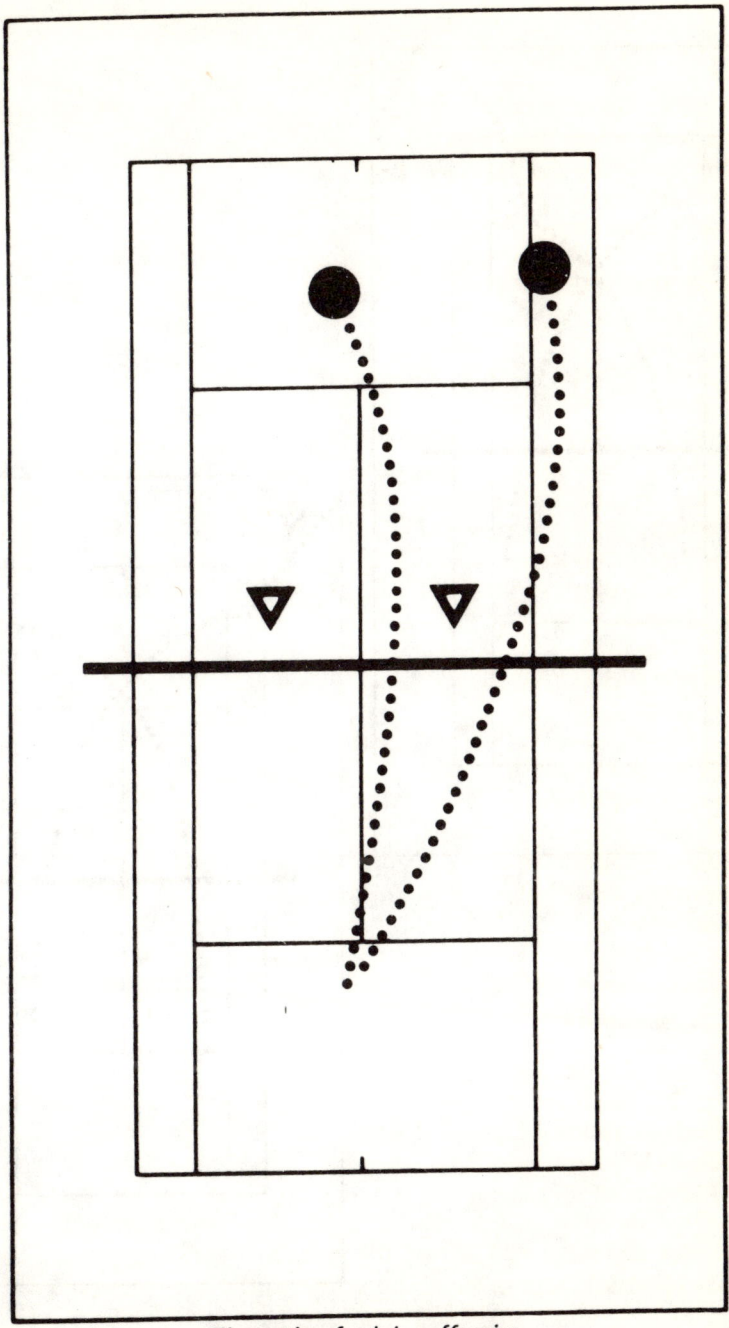

*Illustration for lob - offensive
and defensive (off the wire)*

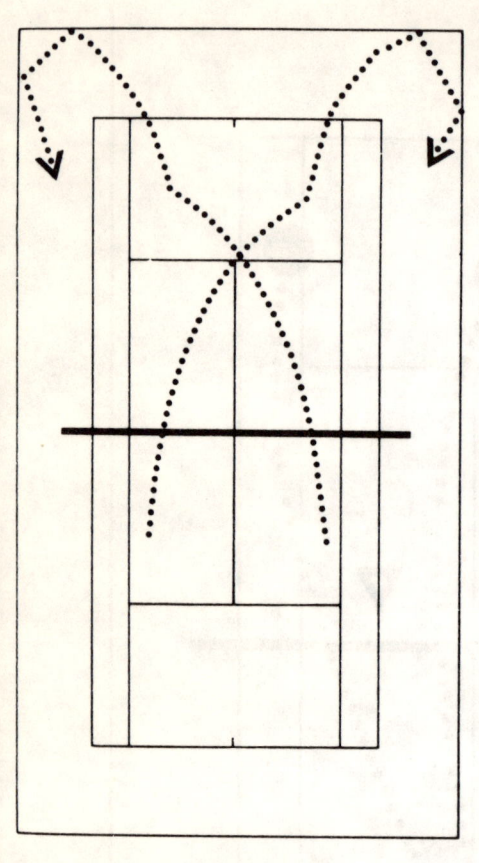
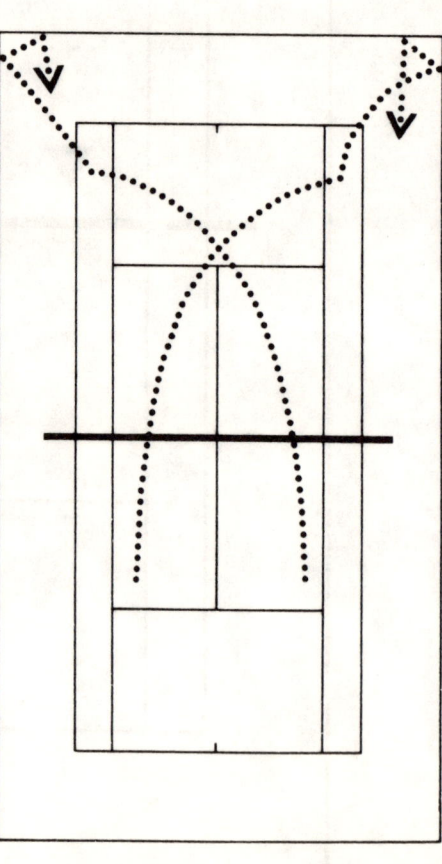

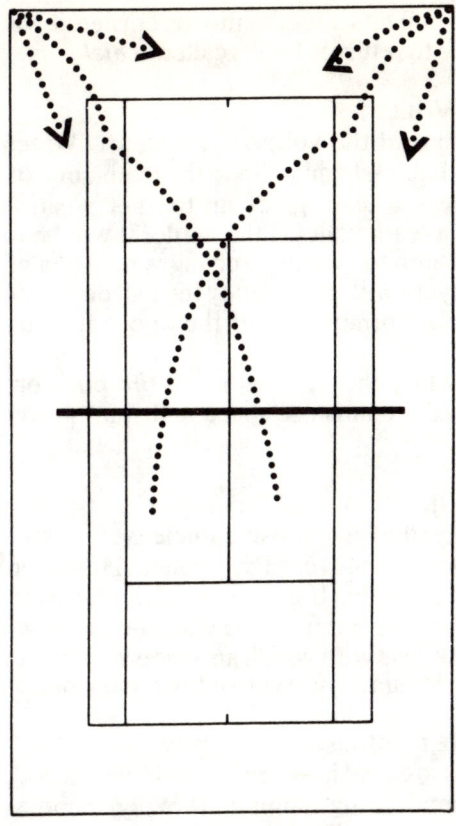

The target areas of the Short Lobs Overhead Return

corners, the corner itself (if the ball hits directly into the corner, it will fly out and be almost impossible to return). This is called a *nick*.

Volley

The young players have honed the volley to a fine art. Watch their lightning-fast reflexes and quick hands. Since the team controlling the net controls the game, no team gives up the net position without a fight; and the better a team volleys, the harder it will be to drive the ball *through* them. Watch for volley exchanges between all four players at the net. Top players will try to volley the ball deep into their opponents' court, near the corners. But if the opponents are deep, a drop volley may be hit.

The point to remember is that the net position is *the* position. Watch the battle for the net as the teams use speed and spin, power and patience, touch and agility.

Wire Play

A wire shot is usually played as a defensive maneuver when a serve, drive, or overhead has been hit through a team. However, some wire shots will be hit offensively. If any serve, drive or overhead is hit too hard it will rebound far out from the wire and may then be driven back. Watch the quickness with which an aggressive player hits this type of shot and how the team moves with it toward the net.

The Paddle

Paddles for platform tennis are oval in shape, made of hardwood, often maple, or metal, the metal being aluminum. Wood paddles usually have a metal or tough plastic binding or rim to protect the edge and are finished in a mahogany shade. A quality paddle costs from $20 to $30.

Holes are drilled through the paddle surface to lessen air resistance when you swing and to make it easier for you to impart spin to the ball. In the standard paddle, there should be from 52 to 74 holes, each three-eighths of an inch in size, arranged in from 8 to 10 rows. What you want to avoid buying is the paddles with fewer holes or models in which the holes are drilled in a U-shaped pattern. A paddle of this type is for paddleball, a very different sport.

Up until fairly recent times, paddles were sold in different lengths. But the standard paddle is now 17 inches long, including the handle which is 6⅝ inches in length.

Weight is an important factor when buying a paddle. The two

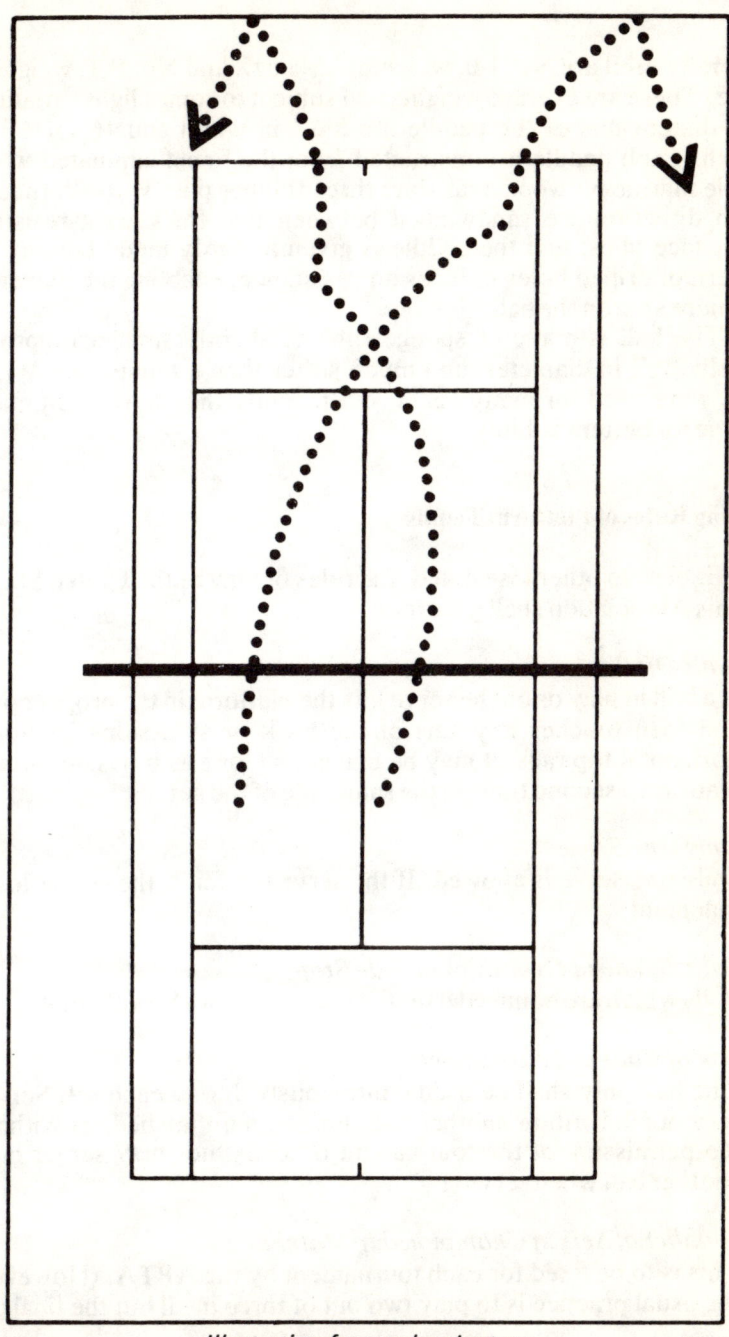

Illustration for overhead return of deep lobs

generally used are No. 1-0, weighing 15¾ oz., and No. P-1, weighing 13 oz. These are average weights and subject to some slight variation. The dimensions of the paddle are 8¼" in width and 16-15/16" in length. Each paddle is constructed from the finest laminated white maple marine plywood available; three thinner plies with alternating grain direction are sandwiched between two thick wear-resistant outer face plies; and the paddle is given a sturdy metal binding. A pattern of drilled holes reduces air resistance, enabling the player to put more spin on the ball.

The ball is made of sponge rubber, slightly smaller (approximately 2½" in diameter) and much softer than a tennis ball. White balls were used for many years, but recently they have been made orange for better visibility.

Playing Rules of Platform Tennis

Except as otherwise noted, the rules of play of the United States Tennis Association shall govern.

1. *Balls Off Wires*
   If a ball in play or on the serve hits the platform in the proper court and then touches any part of the back or side stops including horizontal top rails, it may be played, so long as it has not hit the platform a second time on the same side of the net.

2. *Only One Serve*
   Only one serve is allowed. If the serve is a fault, the server loses that point.

3. *Balls Bounced Over Back or Side Stops*
   Balls which are bounced over the wire result in a loss of points.

4. *Use of Balls in Tournaments*
   One ball only shall be used continuously during each set. Server may not substitute another ball during an unfinished set without the permission of the tournament officials, nor may server hold another ball when serving.

5. *Number of Sets in Championship Matches*
   This is to be fixed for each tournament by the APTA. (However, the usual practice is to play two out of three in all but the finals of

Tribuno men's events.) The finals are three of five sets for men, two of three for women.

6. *Footfaults*
The server shall, throughout delivery of the service, up to the moment of impact of paddle and ball:
a. Not change his position by walking or running.
b. Not touch, with either foot, any area other than that behind the baseline within the imaginary extension of the center mark and the sideline.
NOTE: The server shall not by the following movements of his feet be deemed to "change his position by walking or running":
Slight movements of the feet which do not materially affect the location originally taken by him.
An unrestricted movement of one foot, so long as the other foot maintains continuously its original contact with the deck.
Leaving the deck with both feet.

7. *Good Return*
It is a good return . . .
a. If the ball touches the nets, posts, cord or metal cable, strap or band, provided that it passes over any of them and hits the ground within the court.
b. If the ball, served or returned, hits the ground within the proper court and rebounds or is blown back over the net, and the player whose turn it is to strike reaches over the net and plays the ball, provided that neither he nor any part of his clothes or racquet touch the net, posts, cord or metal cable, strap or band or the ground within his opponent's court, and that the stroke be otherwise good.
c. If the ball be returned outside the post, either above or below the level of the top of the net, whether or not it touches the post, provided that it hits ground within the proper court.
d. If a player's racquet passes over the net after he has returned the ball, provided the ball passes the net before being played and be properly returned.

chapter 9

Building a Platform tennis court

ONE OF THE MORE INTERESTING THINGS about the game of platform tennis is that you can spend a very interesting and useful summer building your own court. In today's market, the construction of a platform tennis court on your property by a commercial builder will probably run around $10,000 at 1978 prices with, of course, variants from area to area. Since most of the platform tennis courts in the country are in the northeast where construction costs tend to be the highest, it can be safely assumed that the $10,000 figure is optimistic.

There are several commercial contracting companies which have made a specialized business out of building courts for platform tennis, the most famous of whom is probably John Reilly. However, there is no real need to spend this kind of money for a court. Almost all of the labor costs, which are the most expensive portion of the construction work, can be eliminated if you and your family are willing to do the labor yourselves. Plans for the construction of a platform tennis court may be obtained simply by writing to the American Platform Tennis Association, c/o Fox Meadow Tennis Club, Wayside Lane, Scarsdale, N.Y. A set of detailed plans and specifications for constructing a court may be obtained for $35.00.

Naturally, all of the materials will have to be purchased, but a family can probably build its own court for about $3,500 under normal conditions, exclusive, naturally, of the land on which it is built. The land required should be about 40 feet wide and 70 feet long to provide the clearance and access required.

All of the prices which have so far been quoted are completely exclusive of lighting. Night court tennis has become much more popular in recent years and, obviously, allows for a much greater flexibility in the use of the court. It is recommended that lighting be included when you build a court. It is almost mandatory that provisions for its later inclusion be made when the court is constructed even if you don't intend to have lighting as part of the original building project. If the provisions for conduits and outlets are made in the original construction, the actual expense of installing the lighting units will be reduced when they are added later.

The cost of an outdoor lighting system for your court is difficult to estimate. This doesn't vary so much from area to area of the country as it does to the taste of the builder. There are several different types of lighting systems which work effectively and such systems as vapor lighting might be considered in certain regions of the country. The best advice here is to consult with a local lighting contractor as to what type of system he recommends for your area, keeping in mind that the purpose of the lighting is to illuminate the court sufficiently that the small platform tennis ball can easily be seen and followed by the players. When the lighting is installed, it must be kept in mind that the angle of the lighting fixtures should be arranged in such a way that they result in the minimum of interference with play and the least possible direct light into the eyes of a player looking up for a shot coming off the wire. It is a wise idea to test position the lighting units before permanently affixing them, just as is done with theatre or ballpark lights.

A couple of other points must be made before we proceed further with the discussion on how to construct your own court. It should be abundantly clear that a poorly-constructed court is a bad investment. For what might be saved through the use of inferior materials and/or shoddy workmanship, the loss of the use of the court once additional repairs and maintainence are being made, plus the cost of those repairs, will more than devour any saving in the initial building costs. Well-built platform tennis facilities can be used not only for platform tennis in the winter (or even summer if one is inclined to play the game on summer evenings) but also for a variety of other family activities. These include badminton, table tennis, gymnastic exercises, children's play area and even picnics and other such family get-togethers.

It should also be noted that since the late 1960's, a small number of platforms have been built of steel and aluminum rather than wood. However, wood of a high quality is still the most popular material for platform tennis court construction and there is no substantial information to indicate that alternative materials are superior in durability or as a playing surface. We, therefore, shall confine ourselves to the construction of a platform from standard wood.

The wood which has been proven consistently to be the best for platforms is kiln-dried deck lumber, normally in thirty-foot lengths.

The type of wood to use elsewhere in the construction can usually best be advised by a reputable local lumberyard. Bear in mind, however, that kiln-dried lumber (or any type of wood, for that matter) will absorb moisture until it has reached roughly the average level of the moisture in the atmosphere to which it is exposed. Excessively dried wood, therefore, is likely to swell somewhat after construction is completed and wood which is underdried may shrink a bit, causing problems with the joining points on the platform. This, naturally, applies to wood used for any type of construction, but is particularly important to take into consideration with a platform since the evenness of the court is paramount to good tennis.

It is not usual to build concrete footings or foundations for platforms, but it is certainly permissible to do so, and might even be prudent to do so, in certain parts of the country. Some platforms have been built with small shaft footings into which the corner posts can be inserted and, conceivably, removed at some point if the platform is to be moved, say, in the event that the owner sells his property.

A platform may be built anywhere, but it should be situated so that the sun's rays do not shine into the eyes of the servers. Since platform tennis is primarily a winter recreation, it is recommended that the platform face a northwest-southeasterly direction. In the event that it is desirable to have accommodations for spectators, these should be built higher than the court.

This way, the spectators are able to look down at the court and see the placement of the shots and returns. Of course, many private courts have little, if any, spectator seating. But experience has shown that it is usually wise to provide some place for other players and their families, friends, and neighbors to watch the action. It is also useful to build the platform within reasonable distance of a house, or some form of shelter, since the game is primarily a winter one. This will also make the drawing of power lines for lighting systems easier and less expensive.

Since the players must constantly be looking up for balls coming off the wire, it is a good idea to avoid as much as possible shading from trees and buildings since they will create shadow patterns, making it difficult for the players to follow the ball, especially in games played in natural light.

A regulation platform tennis court is 61 feet in length and 31 feet in width. The surrounding wire on the sides and backstops is 12 feet from the base of the playing surface. The boards constituting the playing surface should be 30' 6'' in length and join at the net in the center of the court. Standard courts are all built with 2" x 6" boards on the deck flooring. Your construction job will require 128 of these 2" x 6" boards for the court surface. The floor is supported by the four corner posts, two other posts in the middle of each end of the court and four others on either side, or a total of 16 posts. These may be of any size suitable for the terrain.

Normally, the support posts are at least eight inches high, some being higher, others lower to compensate for rises or dips in the building site. The dimensions can best be determined after consulting with your lumberyard. Once the plot has been chosen the side posts should be lined up in a row of six, the center of each 12 feet from the next one. The total length from the end of the first post to the end of the sixth is 61 feet.

Once these posts are in place, an identical row of six exactly parallel should be installed 31" distant. Again, the 31" is measured from the center of the first posts to the center of the second posts. When both parallel rows of support posts are in place, draw a line between the two at one end. Divide this line into three equal segments. At the end of the first and second segments (10' 6") two more posts should be installed to provide the support for one end of the platform. The same procedure is then followed at the other end of the platform. You have now installed 16 support posts and are ready to begin the actual construction of the court.

Generally, two 2" x 6" boards are used for the support or trusswork underneath the court. These should be connected to the support posts so that a set of four double pairs of cross pieces go from the two opposite sets of posts to the other and one inside of the four posts at either end. In the event that the terrain upon which the platform is being built is uneven or unstable, an additional truss post may be added at the midpoint of the inside two crosspieces.

Naturally, caution must be exercised to make certain that these crosspieces are completely level and that they are exactly flush with the tops of the support posts to which they are fastened. They may be fastened by bolts which allow for longer life and better adjustment to the natural changes in the size of the wood than does nailing. Use a standard carpenter's level to check each of these crosspieces before they are bolted into place.

Once these crosspieces are in place, work may begin on the basic flooring of the court itself. The 2" x 6" floor boards are fastened directly into the crosspieces. Under normal circumstances they may be simply nailed into place, but it is advisable not to use nails with too large a head since they may affect the bounce of a ball or the footing of one of the players. Again, your local lumberyard can give more specific advice on this depending upon your particular situation.

Remember, the floor boards are nailed with the 6-inch side serving as the width and the 2-inch side as the depth. They must also be joined extremely close together so that there is almost no room between them. After the first board is in place, the additional boards should be placed next to the one before it and then hammered a bit (no nails!) on the side to drive it completely flush with its predecessor, then nailed into place. Since the 30-foot boards will start at opposite ends of the 61-foot frame, they will not meet in the middle. There will remain a 1-foot gap which will be filled by two boards going in the opposite direction, across the floor.

These two boards will serve as the area of the court directly under the net.

Examination of the official specifications from the American Platform Tennis Association will provide even more complete information on building your court. Their specifications may be used as a virtual blueprint for the construction of the floor.

Once the floor is fastened down, work may begin on the construction of the side and end framework which will support the wire. Place a 2" x 4" support at each corner and then, starting from the first corner, place ten 2" x 4" posts down either side of the platform and four across each end. These figures do NOT include the four corner supports. The total number of uprights is thirty, 11 down each side, with 4 more posts between these at each end.

These posts are supported by an outside crosspiece at the midpoint. The exterior wall is 12 feet in height so that the cross board will be six feet from the bottom end. It should be measured from the bottom rather than the top to allow the full six feet at the bottom since a door must, naturally, be built on one side of the court to permit the entrance of players. Therefore, if a 2-by-4 is used, it will be 6' from the bottom of the frame and 5' 8" from the top from the outer edge of the board on either side.

Additional support for the frame comes at the top of the corner posts where trusspieces are built, forming a triangle with the vertical corner post and the top board going in either direction. The top board, incidentally, is generally inside of the uprights.

The wire itself should be 1" **hexangular mesh with a gauge of** sixteen to insure true bounces and long usage. Make sure that the mesh you buy is galvanized, whether you intend to point it or not.

Crosspieces underneath the platform floor should extend out sufficiently on the sides and ends to allow for the addition of supporting boards for some of the uprights. There is clearly the possibility that an enthusiastic player or players will run into the wire from time-to-time. It is usually advisable to support the four most central uprights on either side of the court and at least two of the four across the end, the two in the middle being the best choices. Sometimes the most central on the ends is supported by a direct piece into the ground but this is optional with the builder or owner.

A door must be built on one side of the court, preferably the one closer to the house or nearest building where the players will be changing, etc. This door should be made of exactly the same materials as the wall it is cut into since, under certain circumstances, balls bouncing off the door could be in play—although this is hardly a common condition. A simple latch or slip bolt will suffice to keep the door closed and it is usually desirable to have a spring or door check on it (on the outside, of course) but, again, this is an option for the builder.

The inside crosspiece around the top of the court should be bolted like the foundation posts and crosspieces but the center support boards and the attached supporting work can be nailed.

When it comes to painting your court, there are a variety of choices. Many owners prefer to have their courts retain as much of the rustic natural wood quality as possible and, therefore, merely varnish their natural wood. Others paint the entire court. If this is the case with your court, the uprights supporting the wire must be painted a dark color, blue or green preferably since light colors make it difficult to see balls coming off the wire.

The court itself, of course, can be painted a somewhat brighter color. Many courts, which are completely painted, have green in all areas except the playing surface itself which is a dark red. Other attractive combinations include natural wood finish to the entire platform except the court which is a light blue. In all cases, of course, the "in-play" area of the court must be painted a contrasting color to the remainder of the platform.

Also, in all cases, the playing area must be marked with two-inch wide white line dividing off the service areas, side lines and end lines.

Three other items worthy of mention are the Evans backstop which gives the end wire resiliency for good rebounds and is included in official plans, hinged snow-boards which facilitate snow clearance where this is needed and 2" collars and 2½" pipes for the nets so that they may be removed easily when the platform is to be put to other use. Regulation platform tennis netting is made of 48-thread tarred cotton with a heavy canvas top binding and taped bottoms and ends. Regulation 2" posts are made of steel and come with cable fittings and reel.